Mindfulness & meditation guided journal

A meditation guide with daily mindfulness journal prompts to feel calm and happy in 30 days.

A Soul Scroll Journal

By Suzanne Heyn

Understand yourself to create a life as unique as you are.

For bonus resources visit:
SoulScrollJournals.com/bonuses

Cover, layout and design by the Soul Scroll Journals team.

For more information, visit SoulScrollJournals.com or email hello@soulscrolljournals.com.

You can also learn more about Suzanne's work at SuzanneHeyn.com.

DISCLAIMER
This book is for entertainment purposes only. This journal is not a substitute for therapy or professional medical or mental health advice.

Although the Author has made every effort to ensure the information in this book was correct at press time, the author does not assume and hereby disclaims any liability to any part for any loss, damage, or disruption caused by this book.

The Author and/or distributors are not responsible for any adverse effects resulting from the use of the suggestions outlined in this program.

Table of contents

Welcome! I'm so excited to start this journey together. It's beyond wonderful that you made an inspiring leap to make the rest of your life the best of your life.

Meditation is a life-changing practice, and over the next 30 days you will taste the boundless peace, joy and deep clarity that's possible with a regular practice.

Keep in mind that meditation is a practice that can have slow rewards. The good news is these benefits are long-lasting, but this practice is a commitment, and it can take time and patience to unravel the rewards.

Have patience with the process and have patience with yourself. Of course it's great to meditate each and every day, but the truth is that you may find yourself skipping days.

Whether life gets busy or resistance wins, things happen. We're only human after all!

The amazing thing with meditation is that over time you will notice yourself in resistance, you will notice yourself prioritizing things other than your inner peace, allowing them to crowd out your spiritual practice, and you will over time make changes, letting those things win less frequently.

But along the journey, give yourself grace. It's okay to be human, to mess up, to do things that don't align with your best interest.

That's why you're here — to learn how to give yourself grace for being human while becoming aware of the ways your humanness is causing suffering. So start now. If you skip a day, just start again.

Please don't use this as an excuse to dilute your dedication, but rather as an incentive to keep practicing and feel compassion for yourself when you fall short.

Just begin again.

Should you use a guided meditation?

There is a guided meditation available to you as a free bonus for purchasing this journal. It's available at SoulScrollJournals.com/bonuses.

However, the true purpose of this journal is to teach you how to meditate on your own, without a guide, so you can access the wisdom of your soul. Guided meditations are wonderful for relaxation, but my intention is to teach you how to navigate your inner world, led only by your own desire and intuition.

This is an essential part of knowing, loving and trusting yourself enough to create a life as unique as you are.

Plan for success

Right now, take a moment and decide when you'll read the first day's lesson and meditate. What day and time? In the morning? Maybe at night, before you go to bed? What obstacles will you need to overcome to meditate?

Plan for them now. Maybe you can prepare tomorrow's clothes and/or lunch tonight, freeing up a precious five minutes in the morning. Or maybe you could set a cell phone reminder for a half-hour before you go to bed, reminding you to meditate.

This isn't about finding time; it's about creating time. It's about showing up for yourself. This is how you learn to love yourself, through creating a relationship with yourself, connecting to your own energy.

This journey is about prioritizing self-care and making sure to serve yourself first so that you can serve others.

Meditation has a way of expanding time, but first you must create time to practice!

To introduce myself, my name is Suzanne Heyn, and I am the founder of Soul Scroll Journals.

I am committed to helping people understand themselves so they can create lives as unique as they are.

I've always been a person who feels things very deeply. A sensitive soul, I was born into a family that didn't understand emotions.

There was no communication, no felt love, no sense of togetherness. So when my father and sister died a year apart from each other while I was an early teen, I created a goal for myself: To appear strong and cold and never hurt.

Maybe I appeared strong on the outside, but on the inside, I felt sad and alone. I spent years at war with myself, wanting to heal my heart and connect with others, but not really knowing how.

Then, at 27, I developed breast cancer. This experience, which I believe partially developed because of my life-long pattern of repressing emotions, broke me open. For the first time in my life, I couldn't repress or deny how I felt. The emotions consumed me.

People told me I was crazy when the truth was, I'd never felt more sane.

While healing emotionally from cancer, I learned to feel my feelings. I developed healing processes to understand what I felt, both the emotions arising from my present experience and those I'd repressed my entire life that were now surfacing.

Many of these processes are outlined here in this journal. Meditation has been one of the most important practices to guide my way forward in life, and I'm so excited to help you connect to your inner voice through this simple, powerful practice.

This is a book of love and understanding. It's a carefully designed journey to guide you home to the deepest part of yourself.

Please commit to the journey and spend time each day with the material and on your meditation cushion. It's easy to resist, but lasting transformation waits for you on the other side. I cannot wait to hear how it goes for you.

Happy soul scrolling!

All the love,

Suzanne Heyn

Founder, Soul Scroll Journals

PS — Share your journaling experience on social media tagging #soulscrolling or @soulscrolljournals for the chance to be featured!

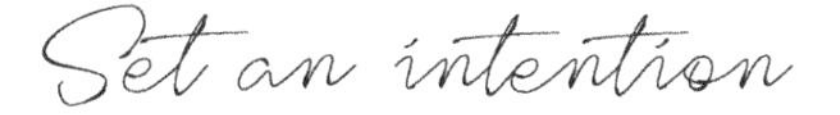

Truly committing at the start of a new adventure can make all the difference between flying through the finish line with enthusiasm and sputtering out half-way through.

Decide right now to commit to the practice and show up! Going through the process is part of the process.

Know that any doubt, fears or resistance you face during the course only reflect the same doubts, fears and resistance you experience in other areas of your life.

This is a spectacular chance to dissolve these blocks for once and for all. Taking a moment to set an intention will help you get better results.

Your intention will be imprinted upon your subconscious, which will help you find the motivation to finish what you started.

1. What is your deepest desire for yourself during this program?

___

___

___

___

2. What will you tell yourself if you grow annoyed, frustrated or contemplate quitting?

___

___

___

___

3. Why do you want this for yourself? Why does it matter?

___

___

___

___

4. Envision yourself at the end of the 30 days. How does it feel knowing you committed and succeeded? What are you thinking now that you're victorious? How has this changed how you see yourself?

___

___

___

___

Feel free to refer to this intention often. Whenever you feel frustrated or doubtful, revisit your desires and allow them to inspire you to continue.

You can do this!

Free meditation for releasing painful emotions

As you go within, things come up. Head to SoulScrollJournals.com/bonuses to access your free meditation to process what you feel and connect to your inner wisdom.

Join the Soul Scroll Journals Family Facebook group!

Personal growth can be lonely, but it doesn't have to be! Head to www.facebook.com/groups/soulscrolljournals to connect with others on the path of creating a unique, soulful life.

A beginner's guide to meditation

Before we begin, a note: It doesn't matter if you read this section before beginning the program. It exists because I wanted the program itself to be more applicable to daily life than a series of frequently asked questions about a seated meditation practice.

That's the purpose of this section: A series of answers to the questions posed to me on social media about meditation.

The truth is, you can't mess meditation up. However you show up is perfect for you. As long as you keep showing up, you'll figure it out. The answers in this section will guide your way, but if you don't feel called to read it, by all means, skip to Day 1 and begin your journey!

Meditation is one of the most profound practices you could ever incorporate into your life.

It helps you develop peace and equanimity, enhances intuition and connects you to your true self. It's profound yet simple, and that apparent contradiction confuses many people when trying to start the habit.

Maybe you've tried sitting and focusing on your breath, but your mind won't stop chattering away, and you think, "This is it? What good is this? How do I quiet my mind and experience peace?"

And then you grow frustrated because your mind won't shut up but now you're more aware than ever of this voice that never. leaves. you. alone. This is where the practice begins: sitting there, with all your chatter and all your thoughts and simply becoming aware of it.

It may seem pointless, like nothing is happening. But you're developing patience and the ability to sit with discomfort. You're developing awareness. Eventually, you will cultivate a part of you who watches these thoughts, who can notice them without identifying with them. As this witness part of you grows, so does your capacity to feel peace in any circumstance.

This happens over time, by simply showing up every day no matter what. (And if you miss a day, simply begin again.)

It's as if the innermost part of your being, your soul, your true self, was the sky, and the thoughts and emotions you notice are the passing clouds. Even if they're sometimes dark, heavy clouds that cause a terrible storm, eventually the sky will clear again.

Don't worry about getting rid of the clouds. Let them move through on their own. Does the sky grow frustrated when a storm comes? No, it simply exists, always calm beyond the clouds and ever-present when the storm blows past.

The storms and the rain have purpose. Perhaps it's a release of atmospheric tension, perhaps it's only a soft rain to nourish parched plants after many sunny days. So too do our own emotions and tears have purpose.

The problem comes when we wish the clouds weren't there, which is resistance, or judging yourself for having rainy days, when they're not only inevitable, but helpful for your ultimate growth.

In human terms, when we judge or resist ourselves, emotional storms last longer. Our resistance stops them from blowing through, leaving clarity and calm in their wake. There's nothing wrong with you for feeling!

This is where the practice starts. Notice your self-judgment and tune into your higher self to recognize that this chatter is natural. As you release resistance and become the observer, you create space for serenity to grow.

In the beginning, you'll need a dash of blind faith that the chatter will quiet and peace will come.

Soon, you'll have the experiences to support this belief and persevering will become easier. For now, allow blind faith to light the way.

Let your heart fill up with the belief in your own potential. Know that everyone experiences these problems. Your task is to sit with whatever arises. Be kind to yourself every step along the way.

Meditation is a practice of learning to accept.

The only way to learn to accept is to sit with what is, especially your emotions. Accepting — and truly feeling — your feelings about a situation is a first step in accepting the situation itself.

It can be very uncomfortable. You may want to run. You may want to numb out, do anything but sit with what is. But as you open up to the things you would rather run from, your heart will expand, your patience will blossom, and your entire life will transform before your very eyes.

You'll become more calm and confident, creative and self-assured. It all comes from a place of being less reactive to what life throws at you and better able to flow with what is.

As with many other things, consistency unleashes the true power of meditation. To experience the benefits, you must commit to a daily practice and show up regardless of whether you feel you're making progress. Changes are happening, they just tend to happen more slowly than we'd like. It's the pace of nature — slow and steady.

The thought patterns and ways of being that you're changing have evolved over decades of life, perhaps even past lives. They take time to unwind. Keep in mind that going through the process is part of the process. Developing the patience to show up no matter what will help you develop the patience to sit through each individual meditation session. As you develop patience to sit in meditation, you develop patience in life.

There is no goal in meditation, no place to go, nothing to do. It's simply a practice of showing up, sitting with what is, and cultivating a habit of responding with curiosity and compassion rather than criticism and judgment.

One day, you'll grow really angry at something, and a part of you will watch yourself flip out and wonder if there's a better way, even in the middle of losing it. And maybe some time after that, you'll notice your anger and then notice space in between your anger and reaction. You'll have expanded your awareness, making it possible for you to feel your anger, breathe into it, accept the discomfort, and respond in a way that doesn't involve flipping out.

Of course, you'll go back and forth between progress and seemingly backwards movement, but, just like the stock market, the dips and rises typically yield a gain over time.

Peace isn't the opposite of chaos. Peace is the process of sitting with chaos until it feels ready to calm down.

Chaos, frustration, tension, messy emotions — these things all have a sacred purpose. They're not things blocking the fulfillment of your desires, but messages from your soul leading you directly there — once you know how to work with them in a healthy way.

Our society has labeled darkness, pain and things that don't fit into neat boxes as 'negative,' 'wrong,' 'bad,' or 'too much.' Sitting with these things will help you reclaim your power. It will make you more confident and certain. Once you face yourself, there's nothing left to fear.

You'll get frustrated. It's fine. You'll think nothing is happening. It's fine. You'll grow annoyed, angry, occasionally feel peace and experience grand epiphanies. It's fine. It's all the same. Notice it, thank it, and sit with it.

As you practice, this will all get much easier. Before we begin, let's dive into some questions.

Q: What is meditation?

A: Meditation is a state of being. It's when your body, soul and mind unite completely with the present moment, when the mind calms and your emotions are at peace. It's a state of being in the flow of the now, when the entire power of your mind is concentrated on the present moment.

Meditation practices and techniques such as guided meditations, walking meditations, directions to focus on the breath or visualize balls of light — these tools merely exist to guide us into a meditative state of being. They're all equal tools.

The technique is not important. Find what works for you, what brings you peace.

That said, know that this experience of peace is something that flowers from consistent practice. I've found it important to practice with the pure intention of showing up rather than with the desire to get something.

When mental chatter arises, don't judge yourself for not being in a state of meditation. Or if you do judge yourself, simply acknowledge the judgment and allow yourself to find humor in it.

Acknowledge that you're in the right place, a place where you can learn to exist in the space between thoughts and emotions. The space where peace is, the space between.

Just as you don't judge your heart for beating, don't judge your mind for thinking. That's what it does, what it's made for. The answer is not to stop practicing, but to practice more. It's not that you're failing because your mind won't quiet, it's just that you haven't sat for long enough.

When someone is enlightened, like Buddha, she or he lives in a perpetual meditative state. The mind is quiet and life is lived fully in the present moment, no past or future. Only now.

That's the promise of meditation. Not even a goal because a goal is something to accomplish. In meditation there is nothing to accomplish, only an intention to be with what is.

I used to worry this would make me boring or lazy or stop me from achieving my goals, but the truth is feeling peaceful makes me feel so much more joyful and relaxed, and living from this place helps me be more creative and productive. Meditation helps me get more done, more joyfully!

In the state of meditation, thoughts quiet. It's very difficult, if not impossible, to be fully aware in the present moment and be thinking. Most thoughts are about the past or future, which means thinking naturally removes you from the present moment.

On another level, most of our perceptions of the present moment result from looking at life through the lens of past experiences or future desires.

We project unhealed past pains of feeling rejected, abandoned or unworthy onto the present moment, essentially reacting as if we were reliving past experiences. We may also project present difficulties through the lens of our future hopes and dreams, perhaps feeling like we'll never succeed because of some present hiccup.

Our reactions are based on the stories we tell ourselves about the present moment, which come from the projections we place upon what's happening. This causes us to resist the present moment and wish it was something different, which creates suffering.

To release resistance, it's helpful to become aware of the stories we tell ourselves, the meaning we attach to things that exists only in our minds.

Because meditation allows us to become present to what is, it helps us identify the stories we tell ourselves, notice when we're telling them, and see what's happening more objectively, rather than through the lens of past and future-oriented projection.

This is the power of becoming present.

Q: What different types of meditation are there? Is one better than another?

A: So many different types exist! There are active meditations, sound meditation, mantra meditation, guided visualizations, breath meditation, focusing on your feelings, chakra balancing meditations... The list is infinite.

The key is to find something that works for you. The technique is irrelevant. What's important is finding something that connects you to your heart, that gives you a tool for sitting with what is until the quiet comes.

Feel free to experiment, and know that just because a type of meditation works for one person doesn't mean it 'should' work for you. Although, I will say that if you experience strong resistance to a particular type of meditation, that could indicate its potential to provide powerful medicine for you.

There's a difference between preferring a specific practice and actively resisting something. The things we resist tend to be the things we need the most. These tend to be the things that hold the most evolution or healing potential on your unique journey.

It's okay to feel resistance, just develop the ability to sit with it so it doesn't control you anymore.

Q: What are the benefits of meditation? What is the point?

A: Meditation brings peace and healing. It strengthens your intuition and helps you grow roots in stillness so that no matter what tornado of chaos swirls around, you stay centered.

Meditation helps you come home to yourself and find your unique way through life. As you meditate, problems literally fall away because you stop attaching yourself to all the drama that circulates both inside and outside of you.

You realize how little life's annoyances mean because everything is so temporary. Meditation gives you perspective and penetrating insight. You develop the ability to pull others into your peace instead of the world pulling you into its chaos.

When bigger problems like death and sickness enter our lives, meditation gives us a place to process our emotions and heal. To connect to the impermanence of existence and understand that no matter how big something is, it too will pass. Because meditation is a practice of letting go, it also helps us face our mortality. As you enter the blackness of nothingness in daily life, you have less fear about what happens when life ends.

When you no longer cling to life, you gain the power to truly live. As you clear space to listen to your inner voice, it becomes your guide along this wild path. You become a passionate creator of your reality rather than someone controlled by fear or things they don't want to feel.

As you heal internally, fewer things bother you. We can only be offended if we believe something is true. Instead of seeking to change the outside — typically a losing battle — you can inquire within to discover why you feel the way you feel and what you really think and believe, the truth underneath the surface of projection-based reactivity.

You gain the ability to appreciate the many layers of life,

including the mix of your perspectives with others' and the truth, which is somewhere in the middle.

In these times of increasing polarity, we need people who are less emotionally attached to their view of right and wrong and more able to sit with the discomfort of disagreement to engage from a conscious place of awareness rather than an unconscious place of reactivity.

This doesn't mean that you allow people to speak to you rudely or lose all your morals. Not at all. But you would better recognize improper behavior and respond in a conscious, empowered way instead of reacting in an unconscious way.

You would respond in a way that reflects your deep connection to the serenity within rather than from a place of being swept away by a riptide of emotion within.

Q: For how long should I meditate?

A: Ideally, it's best to meditate for at least 10 minutes a day, but you can practice for much longer if you desire. At the beginning, the most important thing is to develop the habit without causing too much resistance.

It's a balance, a practice of finding the edge. You want to sit with your resistance, but you also want to be kind to yourself and avoid going crazy, which is easy to do. So if you can sit for one minute, sit for one minute. If you can sit for five, sit for five.

Over time, you will experience benefits and feel more stillness, and this will inspire you to sit for longer. There's no rush. Do more than you're ready for but less than what will cause harm.

Q: Does it always have to be done seated, in a quiet room with the eyes closed?

A: No! Many active meditations exist. This is a program designed to teach seated meditation, and I believe that is the most effective type, but many other ways exist. For example, walking can become a meditation by relaxing into the act of walking. Slowly, mindfully place one foot in front of the other. Notice the birds chirping, the feel of the breeze against your skin. Notice everything around you and merge into the present moment — that's meditation.

Another option is to dance wildly, as hard as you can for 10 or 15 minutes, and then allow your body to sink into seated meditation for another little while.

A third type is knows as the gibberish meditation. For 15 minutes, say gibberish — any nonsensical word or phrase or noise. Say it out loud, moving around however your body moves, and then, for 15 minutes afterward, lay still. Keep your eyes closed the whole time. This sounds really weird, but we did it during my yoga teacher training and some people had very cathartic experiences. It's designed to stir up repressed energy so you can release it.

Technically, any moment you are fully aware and present is meditation. You can meditate anytime, anywhere, even on the busiest street in New York City. But a regular, seated practice helps you grow into that ability.

Q: What should I meditate on?

A: So a lot of times, people, including me, will say, "Meditate on this idea." This practice of sitting with a thought, holding space and seeing what arises is a wonderful way of gaining insight into a circumstance or uncovering a new idea from deep within. But technically, this is not meditation as classically defined as a state of being. (No wonder people get so confused!)

Again, it's not bad to do this and it can be very useful, but it's not meditation. Include it in your practice, but don't limit your practice to it.

Meditation is not a process of sitting with your thoughts or focusing on anything as a goal. It's a process of using focus to relax into the present moment, accepting whatever arises, and opening up to the place inside of you that's beyond the mind. It's a process of expanding rather than focusing, which has a constrictive energy to it.

I think the intention of this question is to inquire about a point of focus — what should you focus on? Indeed, giving the mind a job, to pay attention to the breath or your heart space for example, is a good way to encourage quiet. But the point isn't to focus on either of these things. The point is to create stillness.

Your chosen focus helps to create that stillness rather than being an important factor in itself. It's not what you focus on that matters — it could be your heart or your breath or your belly — but rather the idea of using focus to quiet the mind.

Focusing too much on your thoughts or meditating "on" something can become a trap. It could cause you to stay on a more surface level instead of allowing yourself to expand into a greater experience of peace that lies beyond focus.

As for epiphanies, insights can and will arise, but try to not attach yourself to them. Allow them, notice them, but then release them, returning to a point of focus or the stillness itself.

You can get addicted to these insights: "Look at this epiphany I just had! I'm so smart and spiritual!" But then you get caught in the mind and stay there instead of expanding past the mind. Simply notice this attachment, notice any judgments about it, and keep relaxing into the experience.

I've gone through many meditation sessions attached to my mind and its epiphanies, so don't worry how long it takes. Eventually, as you keep showing up and releasing attachment, your mind will quiet and you will go deeper.

Q: I don't understand how to "focus on my breath." Are you supposed to take deep breaths or just breathe however you breathe?

A: Just breathe however you breathe! You will definitely notice your breath more and this can make it tricky. You might feel like you're short of breath or question how to breath, but that's simply because you're shining your awareness on a normally unconscious process. The idea of focusing on your breath is about simply noticing how the breath feels filling your belly, entering and exiting your nose.

It helps to give your mind something to focus on so your thoughts quiet. Simply watching your breath rise and fall is incredibly relaxing.

When I first started meditating, watching my breath was one of the more difficult places of focus. Besides, I had a lot of unprocessed emotions causing suffering that made it difficult to be in the present moment.

That's how I started focusing on my heart space and sitting with my emotions. There are other benefits to this practice called the Feeling Awareness meditation, which I'll teach you, but one of them is that it's sometimes easier to focus this way.

It's also okay to have more than one area of focus. Ultimately whatever helps you tune into the stillness is the right thing to do for you. The key is to trust yourself and follow your intuition. We're all on different paths, and what works for one person won't work for everyone.

Q: Sometimes I feel silly sitting there. What am I supposed to be thinking or saying?

A: Nothing! Meditation practice is about sitting with yourself, simply noticing what's going on. If you feel silly, that's a great place to start. What does silliness feel like? Where is that feeling in your body? You might also like to journal on it — why do you feel silly?

It helps to have a point of focus, such as the breath, the heart, or a visualization or a mantra, which is a word or phrase. We'll talk about all those things in the coming weeks.

If you feel silly, or notice mental chatter about how you're a fake or a weirdo or silly for believing this stupid habit will do anything for you — who do you think you are, a monk? — just watch those thoughts.

Label them — "Oh that's my friend fear telling me I'm an idiot. Hi fear! Would you like to meditate?"

This is the process of aligning with your higher self, your soul, and over time you'll notice those thoughts and quickly dismiss them as untrue. When that happens, you'll be able to move on very easily.

This practice also helps you notice untrue, limiting thoughts in other areas of life — when it comes to following your dream, for instance. For now, just try to cultivate awareness and remember: Just because it's a thought doesn't mean it's true.

Q: How do I stop the endless mental chatter?

A: The first thing to know is that it's important to keep meditating. Trust that over time, your thoughts will quiet down.

If you're at a point where you feel annoyed by your thoughts, this means you're resisting them. Resistance is fuel that keeps your thoughts going. In this case, you could feel the resistance — literally, what it feels like in your body— or simply continue to bring your awareness back to your chosen point of focus for the duration of the meditation practice, as many times as it takes. As you keep practicing, it will get easier.

Sometimes we keep thinking because we're more invested in figuring out whatever it is we're thinking about than meditating.

In this moment, it's important to recognize this and decide which is more important to you. Maybe it would help you to take a minute and work out whatever it is you're thinking about. Or perhaps you need to re-set your intention to meditate, take a deep breath and refocus.

This happens to me a lot when I'm stressed or worried. I get more committed to figuring out whatever's on my mind than finding peace. In these times, I've noticed that no matter how much I think, I still don't feel better. I've learned to trust that letting go of my problem to relax instead allows me to tap into miraculous solutions.

You'll have to spend time learning how you work and what your habitual responses are so you can give yourself what you need to drop in and feel peace. Start by asking yourself, your intuition —What do I need right now? Create space until the answer comes.

A third option is to expand your awareness so it includes your thoughts, but also everything else in your body. This allows you to stop focusing so much on your thoughts, or whatever it is you're thinking about, and drop more into the present moment. This takes practice, but it will come. Simply become bigger than your thoughts.

You'll often hear meditation teachers say to avoid following your thoughts. This means if you think, "Hmm. I wonder what I should have for dinner," you would ideally notice that thought and then bring your attention back to a point of focus, maybe the breath, the belly or the heart.

Following the thought would involve, for example, contemplating specific recipes you might want to cook or foods you may or may not have in the house. Even if you do end up making a grocery list for 10 minutes, who cares? You showed up, and that's the important part. Trust that over time, your mind will quiet.

The mind's habit is to follow thoughts, and you'll likely automatically begin to contemplate what you would like to eat. It will feel really important. This is probably where you begin to feel resistance. You want to follow your thoughts because you want to solve this problem, but you also want to meditate and find peace. So what do you do? Choose. Choose which is more important to you. Do you want to solve this problem and spend your meditation practice thinking? Or do you want to commit to the practice and feel peace? As you commit, it will be easier to let go.

Then, notice it all. Notice yourself thinking, notice your resistance, your desire to eat. You're expanding your awareness to notice it all. Maybe you'll get caught up in it; that's okay. Simply come back as soon as you notice you're caught up. Over time, practicing this way makes it easier to release the thought without following it. But it takes time.

Today, just sit with the chaos, cultivate compassion for yourself, the one who suffers amid all this noise, and allow your mind go haywire. Just breathe. Try as best you can to focus on your breath, but surrender to the chaos. You spend so much of your energy fighting. It's time to learn how to let go. This is the practice, showing up, sitting here, no matter what happens. Be okay with what happens, even if it doesn't fit your image of how meditation is supposed to be.

We are natural rebels; if we tell ourselves, "Don't think!," we will do nothing but think. This creates resistance and suffering, and meditation is about releasing resistance and suffering. The more you meditate, the more your thoughts will quiet, but don't become attached to that ideal. Keep sitting with yourself, keep showing up, and the rest will come.

Q: If I'm aware that I'm thinking, aren't I still thinking?

A: There's the part of you who thinks and the part of you who observes yourself thinking. The observer is your awareness, your higher self, the force of energy that powers consciousness itself. This is the objective witness that meditation helps us cultivate.

But know that there are two different types of thinking: One type is when you know you're thinking. The other type is when you don't know you're thinking.

The first type is connected to the witness, the impartial part of ourselves that observes everything we do. It's aware that you're thinking and doing it consciously.

The second type of thinking is the type that consumes most of the day. Thoughts, endless chatter. Judgment. Criticism. Worry. Fear. Only most of the time, you're not conscious of it. You're caught up in it. You identify with it, believe every word and consider it to be part of who you are.

This is the source of stress and confusion. This is what meditation helps you become aware of so you can be free. As you meditate, you're thinking, thinking, thinking, and then all of a sudden you think — "Oh my gosh! I've been thinking. I haven't been present at all!" That moment you notice that you're thinking — that's the witness. That's the watcher.

That moment is a victory. This is the part of ourselves we deepen during practice. That's the part of ourselves that embodies peace and love.

As you notice you're thinking, you're learning how to return to stillness. Over time, this muscle will strengthen, and you'll notice you're thinking much more quickly. You'll develop the ability to let the thoughts flow over you, like a river, while you watch from the shore. With practice, you'll stay in this place more of the time.

Q: Ok, but really. How do I quiet my mind?

If your thoughts become a significant problem, you're welcome to recite a mantra a few times to help quiet it down. We talk about this in the program, on Day 11.

Another way to encourage a quiet mind is to meditate after yoga or any other type of physical movement. The physical practice of yoga, asana, was originally designed to prepare the body for meditation, both physically and mentally.

Q: I find it hard to concentrate if traffic goes by or noises interrupt. What should I do?

A: This is a perfect complement to your meditation practice! Life is full of disruptions, and through meditation, we can develop the ability to remain calm in the face of them.

Simply shift your mindset: these noises aren't interrupting you. They're part of your experience and you must work to accept them. They're part of your reality at that present moment.

Expand the container of your awareness so it's big enough to include these noises. Practice sitting with the irritation and this will deepen your peace once the irritation leaves. Of course, it's good to have a quiet place to meditate, but sometimes noises are unavoidable.

Q: I worry that I'm not doing it right. I constantly lose focus.

A: This is why it's a practice! It's not that you're doing it wrong, only that you're building a skill, which is why you have to keep remembering to focus. If you keep practicing, you'll strengthen your abilities. This is the skill the practice is designed to cultivate.

I also really feel like this fear emanates from the deep-seated fear that we are not right, that there is something wrong with us, that there is something wrong with our minds or our souls making us different from others.

We fear we suffer more or have more anxiety or have a more difficult time experiencing this esoteric experience others talk about. We feel like everyone else knows something they're not telling us.

Meditation is about experiencing yourself directly, touching your own divinity, so you know in full faith you are a holy being of infinity.

Meditation, for me, on any given day looks like this: "Okay, sit and breathe. Ahh, this is peaceful. Oh no! I have this idea and this idea and I need to do this thing! Oh no wait! I'm supposed to be meditating. Okay, focus on the breath. Ugh, this is so boring —why am I even doing this?"

It's true. And I have had moments of profound peace, bliss, and deep insights. Those things happen, but they are the exception and not the rule. Most of my practice involves me watching my wandering, sometimes obsessive, sometimes happy, sometimes sad, mind.

Over time, you start to distance yourself from your mind, and even if you barely notice any spaces between thoughts and feelings during seated meditation, you will eventually notice them when you're not meditating.

And that is the true gift. One day you'll be standing in line at the grocery store or sitting in traffic at a red light, and you'll notice yourself breathing.

You'll think to yourself — I am always breathing, and I never notice it. But I just noticed it right now and that's because I sit with myself and my wandering mind and sometimes aching heart. Every day.

Q: How do I create the habit, find the motivation and have the patience to practice regularly?

A: This journal is designed to help with that. :)

But to help you do the work, a few suggestions. First, establish your why through the questions in the beginning of this journal.

Next, create a ritual. Find a specific time of day that works by experimenting with various times. Figure out how you can make more time, whether that's by showering at night to meditate in the morning or spending 10 fewer minutes with technology before bed.

Meditating first thing in the morning is good because not only is your mind the most quiet then, but fewer things can interrupt you. No matter what the day holds, you'll feel satisfied knowing you already practiced.

However, meditation breaks throughout the day are equally useful. A lunchtime session helps you refocus and refuel. An evening practice creates space to release the day.

Don't let your idea of what a meditation practice should look like stop you from creating one that actually works for you.

The act and art of creating this practice in itself is a good motivator because you're doing it your way rather than following someone else's made-up rules.

Another tip is to meditate for a tolerable amount of time. Don't suffer. If you can meditate for one minute, meditate for one minute. Just practice every day. Your sessions will grow longer as your peace increases. Even one minute is better than nothing.

A last tip is to give yourself permission to meditate for varying lengths of time. Some days, I meditate for five minutes and other days I meditate for 20.

Before closing my eyes, I ask myself how much time I want to practice. Some days I'm really busy and congratulate myself for meditating five minutes. It's okay. I showed up.

Deciding before I begin that this day will be a short practice helps me avoid the feeling that I'm failing myself. Instead it feels good, like I'm getting what I need.

On the other hand, sometimes I decide to meditate for 20 minutes, and I stick to this decision even when five minutes passes by and I'm bored already. Sometimes we give ourselves breaks and other times we push through the resistance.

Science is divided upon how long it actually takes to form a habit, but 30 days should be a long enough time for you to experience some benefit from meditating. As you experience small benefits, this will inspire you to continue practicing.

When you find it difficult to motivate yourself, think of why you want to meditate. Hold the image of you, feeling peaceful, calm and joyous in your mind, and allow that image to inspire your continued dedication.

If you don't practice for a day, or a few days, notice yourself growing irritable, stressed, depressed, anxious or angry. Then, compare that sense of irritability with the peace you feel after meditation. Noticing that you feel irritable because meditation has been absent from your life would actually be a great sign! It would mean you're aware enough to recognize that you feel irritable and detached enough from self-judgment to realize why.

Overall, I recommend igniting a burning yes to return to the practice. In life, we're always saying yes to something, even if it looks like a no. Saying yes to meditation is saying yes to living life as the best version of you. Saying no to meditation is actually saying yes to something else — to watching an extra 10 minutes of television, scrolling on your phone instead of your soul or sleeping.

These choices aren't necessarily bad, but notice how your choices make you feel and what kind of a person they're carving you into. Notice the results you get from your choices. Make choices to reflect the kind of person you want to be, and the kind of life you want to live.

If you know who and what you want to become, it will be easier to say yes to meditation. Not because you feel like meditating, but because you want to become a certain kind of person who lives a certain kind of life. From there, the patience will grow.

Q: I would like to have that habit in my daily routine but I always forget or, when I remember, it's when I'm in bed about to sleep.

A: A commitment seems to be in order. If you make a big, grand commitment to meditate each day for 30 days, you will establish a habit, and once you establish a habit, it will be like brushing your teeth — impossible to forget.

If you still need help, I recommend setting a daily alarm on your phone, "remember to meditate." Set an alarm for your designated practice time, and keep this journal on your nightstand so you see it before getting into bed. If you're in bed and remember, simply take five minutes and meditate first. It won't take long, will help you sleep better, and though it seems too minor to matter, the truth is this tiny action helps you create the habit.

If you find yourself engaged in a dialogue like, "I don't really need to meditate. It's not that important," recognize that voice as belonging to your lower self, as opposed to the higher self, and meditate anyway. Reconnect to your why and devote yourself to your higher self. You'll have days where your lower self wins, but keep growing your awareness and your desire to meditate, and over time, the higher self will win.

Q: How do I overcome the resistance to meditation?

A: In The War of Art, Steven Pressfield writes: "Rule of thumb: The more important a call or action is to our soul's evolution, the more resistance we will feel toward pursuing it."

I'll tell you a story about my own practice, but first a quick perspective shift: When I resist meditating, I always tell myself, I have no trouble spending 15 minutes (often much, much more) scrolling on social media or reading or doing any number of things. If I can do any of those things for 15 minutes, I can sit with myself for that amount of time.

Yet, I resisted meditation for four years, and my life shifted so dramatically after beginning that I can only wistfully wonder how life would have unfolded if I'd begun sooner.

Four years is a heavy dose of resistance, so just know that you aren't alone. Also know that if you're seriously resisting the practice, it only signals how much your soul craves it.

My personal journey of overcoming resistance was to keep moving slowly towards meditation, inch by inch. I meditated for one minute, and then three. My practice lengthened over time as I nurtured the ability to sit with myself without going crazy.

If you're resisting meditation, first drop your resistance to the resistance. You know you want to meditate and yet you have this resistance. Your desire and your resistance clash, creating even more resistance.

Accept that you resist the practice. Accept that it's going to be difficult the first little while. And then sit every day, even if only for a minute. The only way to melt resistance is to enter it, sit with it. Show it you're not afraid. Cultivate the courage to show up anyway. Don't hide behind it as an excuse. Meditate anyway!

That said, if you skip practice for a day or a week, don't be hard on yourself. Just return to it as soon as you can. Don't allow your journey towards peace to cause inner turmoil. That defeats the purpose!

Q: I want to learn more about my real wants and needs. How can meditation help me listen more deeply to my heart?

A: Meditation helps you listen more deeply to your heart by helping you connect to the stillness within, your true self. From that stillness, sometimes messages or epiphanies will arise, clearly articulating your wants and needs.

But even if these messages don't arise during meditation, know that spending more time with yourself allows you to deepen your connection to your inner voice. It will come bubbling up as you make decisions and interact with the world around you.

It will give you messages as you respond to other people and situations. You may hear the louder voices encouraging you to respond the way you normally do, but now you will also hear the quieter voice from within expressing what you really want to do.

In those moments, your job becomes to follow the true voice rather than the louder voice reflecting doubts, fears and others' expectations. (If this feels difficult, that's where journaling and shadow work come in.)

Through meditation, you also become more in tune with your emotions, which are messages from your soul. This greater connection will help you understand how you truly feel about the circumstances in your life, and know what you really want.

On an energetic level, meditation allows more spiritual energy to enter your body while cleansing you from heavy past pain. This clearer space and greater connection to your divinity also increases your ability to hear your heart.

When you are full of life force, this creative impulse drives you forward in a way that's unique to you. The more full of life you are, the more you will naturally understand your true wants and needs. This forward propulsion will be irrepressible.

Meditation also strengthens the third eye, the ajna chakra, the seat of intuition. Being in touch with your intuition connects you to an infinitely wise guide dedicated to helping you walk your unique life path and purpose.

Q: Sometimes I feel anguished or nervous while trying to meditate. I always worry about doing other things. It's like my mind resists surrendering. What do I do?

A: First, know that this is totally natural. Many people are terrified of meditating on some level because it's basically an ego death. The mind fears silence because it fears nothingness, just like it fears death. We all fear the unknown, and the silence within is the ultimate unknown.

Know this fear is also an incredible potential because as you grapple with the fear of the unknown in meditation, you'll feel more comfortable with the unknown in every day life.

From a practical perspective, I would start with the fear. What are you afraid of? How does this fear feel in your body? As you meditate, feel the fear. This simple act of welcoming it in rather than resisting it creates space for you to transform it.

Before meditating, you might also write down a list of everything practical you're worried about, any specific fears you have or things you're resisting, including related to meditation. That way, as you meditate and things come up, you can tell yourself, "It's okay. It's on the list. I'll do it later."

As you sit with any nervousness or anxiety, know that it's okay to feel that way. Even if you spend your whole meditation feeling nervous, it's okay! The process is about accepting whatever your reality is at that present moment.

Trust that as you keep showing up, you're unwinding major patterns that will not only help you meditate more deeply, but also enjoy life more fully. You're creating an awareness that will allow you to live based on your true heart-felt desires rather than from a place of avoiding things you don't want to feel.

Week 1: Self-love and compassion

The essence of true life is true love. Self-love is the foundation for creating any new, life-affirming habit.

This week, you'll set a strong foundation for your brand new meditation habit while learning basic techniques.

You'll learn an essential tip to help if you can't sit still and discover why the term "mindfulness," is actually a misnomer.

Day 1: A foundation in love.

Now the work begins. Are you ready? Today is all about setting a foundation and rooting down in love.

Often the desire to create new habits initiates from the false idea that we'll be a better person if we change, if we become more joyful or peaceful. I invite you to start the habit of meditation out of love. Root down in the understanding that you are already enough.

Come to the practice from the desire to love yourself more, to give your soul the love-soaked life it deserves, and not the desire to become a better person. You're already good enough!

The purpose of meditation isn't to change who you are, but to connect to the truth of who you are. To shift your experience of life so that it becomes an expression of your true self, instead of the small self influenced by doubt, fear and resistance.

You are a soul, a slice of infinity sandwiched in skin.

Your body allows your soul to experience life on this Earth, to touch, taste and smell every wonder. Meditation is the practice of connecting to the eternity within your skin. The more you connect, the more effortlessly Earth debris like doubt, fear and confusion dissolves.

These are temporary experiences covering a deep peace that's always available to you, in every moment. To connect to that serenity during difficult moments, all you need to do is practice daily when it's not so difficult.

Meditation opens a clear channel for more spiritual energy to flow through you. It quiets the mind as you practice connecting with your soul.

A quiet mind is a result of meditation, not a pre-requisite. The practice isn't one of taming the mind into quiet submission, but of understanding its true nature and of understanding your true nature.

To quiet the mind, sit. When the mind races with thoughts, simply continue to sit. Have faith that as you continue to show up, stillness will eventually come.

Develop the patience to outlast your thoughts. You are eternity. Connect to that eternity and the passing phenomena of thoughts will soon prove their impermanence.

Know that whatever arises during your practice is all okay. You are worthy of love, you are love, regardless of how you feel. Regardless of whether you feel sad or angry, full of regret for things you have or haven't done. It's all okay.

Meditation is a place to sit with whatever is, and find the peace, find the love. There is love in everything because nothing is all good or all bad.

Keep in mind that the mind isn't all bad.

Thoughts aren't all bad. They may contain epiphanies from heaven above, new ideas, and messages to help you communicate with those around you. Thoughts are simply manifested energy.

The mind creates thoughts because that's what it does, kind of like how the eyes see and the heart pumps blood.

All of our organs have important jobs and the mind's job is to think. So don't hate the mind for thinking or yourself for having a mind that loves thoughts. It's what it does. That would be hating your mind for its nature, for what it is.

Do you hate yourself for who you are? Work to love your mind for what it is and you will begin to love yourself for who you are, and others as they are. Appreciating one thing for what it is helps us appreciate all things for what they are.

Meditation is not opposition to doubt and fear. It's noticing their existence while simultaneously strengthening your connection to your true self, which is your energy. Your soul.

Meditation is the process of breathing in your soul's energy and the universe itself, and allowing it to nourish you. If you're nourished enough, having the occasional french fry of doubt or fear won't kill you!

So today, know that the practice isn't about telling the mind to stop talking or becoming a better person. It's about connecting more deeply to the love you already are.

How to meditate

First thing's first — how do you sit?

The most common posture is cross-legged, sitting with your hips elevated on a pillow or folded blanket. This reduces pressure on the lumbar spine and makes sitting much more comfortable. Sit with a spine that's straight but not stiff.

Place your hands on your knees, palms up to receive energy or down for grounding/calming. If you'd like, touch your thumb tip and index tip together in gyan mudra, which promotes calm.

If your legs become uncomfortable, feel free to extend them straight out in front of you or shift in any way that feels good. It's okay to move during meditation if you need to!

You could meditate lying down, however I don't recommend it. It makes it too easy to fall asleep, which could create the habit of you falling asleep whenever you practice.

Meditation is about tuning in, and not tuning out, so lying down is generally not advisable for a regular practice.

When do you sit?

Sit whenever you'd like, morning, afternoon or night. During this first little bit, allow yourself to experiment with sitting at different times of day, unless you already have a clear idea of when you'd like to meditate or you feel having a designated time is important to help you create the habit.

See what naturally feels good without holding yourself to a specific time because that's what you think you're supposed to do.

Eventually, it'd be good to find a regular time that works, but for now, I invite you to give yourself the freedom to experiment with non-traditional options. Tune in to your higher self and see what your intuition recommends.

Where do you meditate?

It can be nice to have a dedicated meditation space, but you can also simply sit in your bedroom, outside, or any other area you'd like. There literally are no rules! It's all about what feels good for you.

Creating a special meditation area decorated with candles and any statues or crystals you enjoy is nice, but absolutely not necessary. Do it when you feel called to, not because you think you should.

Tips for today's meditation

Feel free to explore the guided meditation at SoulScrollJournals.com/bonuses or simply sit with yourself for any amount of time that feels good to you. Even as little as one minute!

As for meditation timers, I like Pocket Meditation Timer for iPhone. Many people also like Insight Timer.

Over the next 30 days, you'll learn how to breathe, what to focus on, and much more. If you're not sure of something, trust the process! The answer will come. You can also ask in the Soul Scroll Family Facebook group linked to on the bonuses page.

Overall, I encourage you to begin to have faith that as long as you show up for yourself, you literally cannot go wrong. Go within and see what feels right! As you sit with any uncertainty, you will learn to trust yourself. Enjoy the journey within!

Journal prompts

How did today's practice go for you? In what ways did you judge it as good or bad, or feel unsure? How could you see it instead?

Consider writing yourself a love note for all the ways you're proud of yourself for showing up in meditation and in life.

Day 2: Move first.

Welcome to Day 2! I hope you enjoyed sitting yesterday! Keep showing up! The first few days of creating a new habit are the hardest.

Today's message is a bit more practical: Move first!

This will come in handy for those of you who struggle with restlessness. You'll also learn tips to turn any movement or activity — washing dishes, even — into a meditation.

Restlessness or feeling like you can't sit still is a common problem for meditators. That's why moving meditations, which we'll talk about in a minute, are so popular. If that idea resonates with you, I encourage you to try.

First, let's dive deeper into ways of making a seated practice work despite any restlessness.

One of the easiest ways to promote a calm body and mind during seated meditation is to preface it with yoga.

Asana, the physical practice of yoga, was originally designed to prepare both the body and mind for meditation. Yoga strengthens the spine and opens the hips to make sitting on the floor easier. It removes restlessness and, after an hour of focusing on the breath while moving, the mind much more easily drops into peaceful stillness.

When you think of it this way — a full hour of yoga prepares the mind to meditate — it makes sense that we have difficulty quieting the mind when just plopping down after a busy day. (This is another reason why morning meditation tend to be good. The mind is quiet, not fully awake.)

During yoga teacher training, my teacher encouraged us to end all our classes with a brief seated meditation. She lamented that so often, we do all the preparation work and then stop moments before enjoying the full fruits of our labor, allowing the peaceful glow of the practice to fill every cell of the body.

If you don't practice yoga, or if you just feel like trying something new, I invite you to try dancing for 10 or 15 minutes before sitting. Turn on your favorite song — try to find something that encourages you to move, but mellow enough to avoid over-stimulation — and dance.

Try different types of dancing, maybe shaking your hips and moving every part of your body totally uninhibited. You might also enjoy more mellow movements, moving your arms around like branches in the breeze and simply exploring the space around you.

Keep moving, past the point where you feel like stopping. This is the secret to quieting the body, pushing past your initial limit. Tire the body out.

Once you stop dancing, turn the music off and come into a seated position to focus on your breath for however long you decide to meditate.

Another option is to go to the gym first. Do cardio for 30 or 45 minutes, wear yourself out, and then meditate.

The secret is to work with your nature instead of against it.

Us modern day humans sit way more than nature intended. Many of us don't exercise nearly enough, and it's natural that we're restless. We don't move enough. Meanwhile, our stress responses are on overdrive, leaving our bodies filled with amped up stress hormones.

Give yourself time to quiet down. Burn off those stress hormones through exercise. Then try to sit.

If you don't move directly before practicing, at least exercise at some point during the day. Making sure you're getting enough exercise will help you embrace the stillness.

Transforming movement into meditation

If you absolutely can't sit still, transform movement into meditation. Runners frequently report a runner's high, and this sometimes results from experiencing God. The runner disappears and only running is left.

Walking meditations are also popular. If you choose to walk or run to meditate, I encourage you to refrain from listening to music. Listening to music while doing another activity is technically multi-tasking. Seek quiet.

Even if you do have a seated practice, the techniques outlined here will help you add a meditative quality to everything you do.

The first step is to set the intention to meditate. Sometimes it's nice to walk or run to be with your thoughts and think things over. That has value, but it's not meditation because meditation isn't a time to think. It's a time to be.

So thoughts will arise of course, because that's what they do, but have the intention that this is a time to meditate and not a time to think.

Instead of giving your awareness totally to your mind, give it to the world around you. Stand for a moment before you start moving, noticing your feet firmly on the ground beneath you. Your spine straight and tall, your heart open.

As you begin walking, notice the weight of your legs moving through the air. Notice your feet hitting the pavement below, the weight shifting from the heel to the ball of the foot as you move. Notice the air on your skin, any scents permeating the air. Notice the beautiful colors of the sky, any birds or animals around you.

Notice your energy. Feel whether it's frantic or calm, anxious or settling down. Connect to it. Connect to the world around you. Breathe and notice yourself breathing. Expand your awareness to include your inner and outer worlds, the world within your body and the world outside your body.

If thoughts arise, notice them, thank them, and then consciously return your awareness to the present moment. The thoughts will keep coming, and that's okay. Let them swirl around you and over time, they will quiet. Simply keep the intention, this is a time for meditating, and you will soon feel more at peace.

If you feel bored, notice the boredom, notice thoughts related to the boredom, that this is a stupid practice and you have better things to do. Notice those thoughts and then align with your higher self, the one who wants to meditate and experience peace. Connect again to your intention and allow that to motivate your continued practice.

These methods apply to all activities. Make washing the dishes, folding laundry or even mopping the floor meditative. Allow yourself to drop totally into the action and cultivate fascination for the things most people barely think about. (Water coming from the faucet! Water rushing over your hands. Molecules mixing and the sacred action of cleanliness happening.)

Tips for today's meditation

Move first! Do whatever activity feels good to you, whether yoga or dance or a walk outside. Turn this activity into a moving meditation. You may also choose to sit in stillness for a few minutes afterward. Notice your energy percolating through your body.

Journal prompts

What did you notice happening in your mind as you practiced a moving meditation? How did this increased mindfulness transform your experience? What's one area of life where you'd like to set the intention to pay more attention? Why does this matter to you?

Day 3: Adopting a growth mindset.

Welcome to Day 3!

When something is hard for you, what thoughts form? Do you tell yourself that you'll never be good at this? That some people have it and some people don't, and apparently, you just don't?

Thoughts like this are destructive because they make people give up. To transform this mindset, consider cultivating curiosity instead and setting the intention to enter the discomfort and grow.

One of meditation's greatest gifts is becoming more aware of all the ways we sabotage ourselves, of shining greater awareness on our thought patterns and creating space between thoughts and our reactions. In this space, we can recognize which thoughts serve us and which don't, which thoughts represent our true boundless nature, and which don't.

As you exercise this judgment, you gain the ability to select which thoughts you believe and which you want to ignore.

The practice of meditation in itself will help you take your thoughts less seriously, but today's discussion is about examining your relationship to meditation and seeing how that relationship mirrors difficulties in other areas of life.

Do you resist meditation? Why? What don't you want to experience or face? What do you think you'll find? Do you think peace is not for you? Are you expecting immediate results and rewards from a practice that moves at a sometimes glacial pace?

When you start to think meditation is stupid, or that you'll never be able to experience peace, become aware of the thought and then consciously align with your higher self.

The higher self is the self who knows everything is possible. The self who bought this journal and showed up to do the work. Begin to identify with this higher self more.

Tell yourself that although you may not currently have the ability to easily sit, you're developing that ability every moment that you continue despite the discomfort.

This simple process of noticing your thoughts and then questioning them supports this increased alignment with your higher self, the pure awareness of you. The simple act of noticing creates space to shift.

It may feel like nothing is happening as you practice, but the act of noticing and questioning is building a muscle that strengthens over time. The pace of meditation is slow.

In our modern, fast-paced world, people often want instantaneous results. Can you commit to this practice for the long-haul? Continue to show up even when it feels like nothing is happening?

Can you trust that as you keep showing up again and again, you will shift and your experience of meditation will deepen?

This perspective shift is known as a growth mindset. A growth mindset says, "I am not currently able to do this thing, but if I keep showing up and practicing, I will eventually develop the skill."

A non-growth mindset says, “I’m horrible at this and I might as well stop trying because I’m never going to get better. It's not working."

It sounds obvious, but many of us need to consciously adopt a growth mindset. Face-to-face encounters with your shortcomings can be difficult. It’s where most people give up. But by sitting with the discomfort of feeling like you’re failing, you’re expanding in so many ways.

You’re expanding your ability to sit with discomfort, which is in itself valuable and will expand your peace. But you’re also expanding your mindset.

Just because something is not possible or easy today doesn’t mean it won’t be possible or easy tomorrow. And when you finally do expand your ability, the satisfaction will feel so good.

Keep showing up. Let repetition be your effort. Tell yourself that you’re growing and changing. Ignite the fire of blind faith and let it fuel your journey until experience backs it up.

Incredible peace waits for you on the other side of any discomfort.

The true magic of meditation isn't the beautiful colors or mystical experiences that some people report. The magic is the practice's ability to transform you, molecule by molecule as you show up breath by breath.

The magic is meditation's ability to wipe away stress, fear and past pain that leaves you reactive and unable to enjoy your life. One day someone will provoke you and an incident that may have previously destroyed you for moments or hours or days will not rock you from your center.

At that moment, you'll realize you changed. All those moments that felt like nothing added up and you have somehow become more you — the you that you always wanted to be, but weren't sure how.

All because you believed in yourself and kept showing up. That's the magic.

Tips for today's meditation

Notice how you feel about the practice itself — including resistant, anxious, afraid or bored. How do those feelings feel in your body? Simply sit with them. Notice any related thoughts that arise.

Journal prompts

Think about any resistance or anxiety you have toward meditation. What is that about? If you're not sure, tune into the emotion and free write from that place. In what ways does this parallel how you relate to other things in life?

How do you respond when things feel hard? What do you tell yourself and what do you do? How would you rather respond? What would you need to believe in order to respond that way?

____

____

____

____

____

____

Day 4: Love your crazy mind.

Over the past few days of sitting in meditation, you've likely become much more acquainted with all the thoughts running through your mind.

You already know that not all of these thoughts are true, and since you're meditating, you'd probably like to quiet those thoughts down to feel more peace.

The desire for peace is an amazing desire to have, but with desire comes resistance — even with a desire as seemingly pure as peace. Attaching to desire creates distance between the present moment and the moment we wish was reality.

It's okay to desire, it can be wonderful motivation — the desire for peace and fulfillment brought you here — but expand your capacity to hold that desire in awareness while simultaneously accepting the present moment.

The key is to allow your thoughts and feelings to coexist with your desire for peace.

Expand your awareness to include them. It's okay to think. The problem doesn't come from thinking itself, but thinking that thoughts are a problem.

This creates resistance, which feeds the thoughts. This entire process of meditating is about accepting everything exactly as it is — including your thoughts, emotions even resistance.

Accept that your thoughts exist, remove the resistance to them, and simply move your awareness back to your body or breath. Setting the intention to release the resistance will help mute the chatter. Root down in any bodily sensations and explore the inner world of your energy.

Two different types of thinking exist

The endless chatter is unconscious awareness, one type of thinking. This surface chatter is essentially a first layer of dust covering up your true, expansive self. Have patience with this dust, sit with it, and eventually it will clear away.

Then, there's the voice judging the chatter. That's a second type of thinking. This second type is closer to the higher awareness that you'd like to connect to.

Remove the energy of judgment from the second type of thinking, the voice judging the chatter, because you have more control over it.

Replace judgment with compassion for yourself, the one living with this endless stream of unconscious chatter.

Allow the thoughts to hum in the background. Quiet comes when you accept that the thoughts are there and sit long enough for their momentum to slow on their own. These thoughts are fed by the fuel of resistance. What you resist, persists!

As you sit in the stillness and enter the now, and as you consciously remove resistance, the thoughts begin to run out of fuel. They slow down and eventually stop. There's simply nothing to feed them anymore. Have faith that they'll slow down.

Some days, your mind will race the entire time. It's okay. The most important things is that you showed up and continue to show up. It may feel like nothing is happening, but it is!

You're changing your relationship with your thoughts, training yourself to observe them instead of react to them. This is deep work and takes time. Trust the process.

If doubt arises, respond with compassion and affirm your commitment. We can spin ourselves down deep roads. You might have doubts, then judge the doubts, then worry that this meditation thing will never work because you're judging the doubts. It's okay.

At any moment, you can interrupt the cycle with compassion and presence. At any moment, you can exhale and let it all go. Return to your chosen point of focus, whether the breath or belly or guided audio.

And then, at some point, the thoughts will start in again. This is the process. Dropping thought, thinking, noticing you're thinking, dropping thought. Over and over again, like training a very young, very stubborn puppy.

It seems like it's pointless, like nothing is happening, but this is the practice! Meditation may be the stillness, but it's not something to achieve. You'll fall into meditation naturally once you sit with your thoughts long enough for them to slow down on their own.

Thoughts are like a wind-up doll that will eventually run out of juice. Sit with them long enough and you will experience peace. This entire process will build patience in you.

You must cultivate more patience than your stubborn puppy of a mind.

Some days and some periods of your life will be more turbulent than others. That's okay. The most important thing is that you keep showing up.

Consider that becoming aware of your chatter is progress. All day long, your mind chatters away, but you're so identified with it that you barely notice. So when you sit, and the mind keeps talking, you've become aware of its ever-present commentary. This is the first step!

This newly developed awareness that the mind is talking, this is the same awareness that will develop as you sit in stillness every day. And over time, that awareness expands and you identify with it more than the chatter. When you identify more with the awareness and less with the chatter, the chatter will quiet.

It's truly that simple.

The mind is not the enemy. We don't sit to kill our thoughts. We sit to find peace. Fighting something only strengthens it. Killing things is for crazy people.

Tips for today's meditation

Today, focus on accepting your thoughts instead of resisting them. Accepting doesn't mean investigating them or analyzing them, but simply letting them exist. Letting them do their thing without your participation.

When you judge yourself for thinking or judge the thoughts themselves, thank the mind for its input and summon self-compassion. Love your mind because it's part of you and has a valid contribution to your life. Recognize that your mind is just doing its job.

Expand your capacity to be aware of your thoughts while simultaneously becoming aware of the present moment and your chosen point of focus, the breath, the heart, the belly.

Don't allow the presence of thoughts to make you think you're failing at meditating.

That's so silly! It makes me laugh even writing it. You can't fail at meditation because all meditation is, is tuning into the pureness of the present moment.

Right now, you're thinking! And that's okay. Simply notice that you're thinking and don't worry about it too much. The less energy you give your thoughts, the sooner they'll quiet.

Visualize yourself sitting while your thoughts flow like a river above your head. Visualize space and space will be created.

And for the rest of the day, even when you're not in meditation, check in every so often. What are you thinking about? What is the quality of your thoughts? How attached to them are you?

Journal prompts

What is your relationship with your mind? Do you fight your thoughts or accept them with love, curiosity and compassion? What would you like your relationship with your thoughts to be?

____

____

____

____

____

____

Day 5: the truth about mindfulness.

Today we're talking about mindfulness, which classically refers to present moment awareness. The ability to live fully in the present moment with a quiet mind and peaceful heart. This of course is the purpose of meditation, to teach us how to dwell in that place.

However, the word "mindfulness" is actually a misnomer because what we're really practicing is the ability to go beyond the mind, to connect to that empty place where only pure awareness lies.

We humans are attached to the idea that we need our minds for everything. The mind is a wonderful tool that we can use to analyze information, contemplate life and plan things. We rely on it, thinking it makes us safe. It actually traps us in limitation, the illusion of control, and the stories we tell ourselves that handcuff our potential.

In truth, we're scared of space and thoughts help us fill that space.

We're scared of surrender and clinging to our thoughts protects us from experiencing the free fall of connecting to nothingness.

Thinking removes us from the present moment and propels us into the past or future. If we're thinking, chances are we're not in the present moment. Our mind is full, but we're not being mindful.

We're so used to using the mind for everything that we stop searching for the more subtle signs in life, the ones that come from our intuition, the world around us, and through non-verbal communication.

In meditation, many people wonder, what should I think about? Because it seems weird to have a mind empty of thought. What is the point? What happens beyond thought? What is emptiness?

Beyond thought is awareness, pure consciousness itself. The infinite source of life, creativity, ideas, and the universe. The source of everything. The source from which everything, including the mind itself, came.

The more we quiet the mind through practices like meditation and allowing ourselves to flow and feel more, think less, the more life force energy we receive.

The thing is, this presence is always there, always available to us. But we're afraid of its emptiness and block it with our thoughts, with our desire to control. Sitting in meditation is really a practice of letting go. Of increasing our ability, breath by breath, to stomach the intensity of entering the void.

Can you handle the power of entering nothingness? Of touching with your heart the source of all that is?

The more we connect to this place beyond mind, the less we need the mind.

We actually don't need to think as much as we do. How many decisions are made more difficult because of thought? You debate what you should or should not do, when in your heart you already know the answer. The mind is useful, but it also complicates things. When you identify with your doubt, you doubt yourself.

It's fine to doubt and fear, just stop identifying with it.

When you go beyond mind, you empower your connection with divine intelligence to guide your life. As your confidence in this connection-fueled co-creation increases, so does your ability to live more mindlessly, but more heart-fully. You become more tuned in to the natural flow of all that is.

And so meditation increases so-called mindfulness, but it's actually a practice of connecting to the place beyond mind. Become mindless, but overflowing with connection to that place beyond. Surrender to the fear that comes from entering the void.

You don't need the psychological complexes you've adopted to keep you safe. You don't need to doubt yourself or your intuition. You don't need to question whether you're smart enough or good enough.

Drop into the void, surrender to it. As you overcome your fear of it and everything that blocks you from experiencing it, you will become fearless.

There's a saying: "Fear is excitement without the breath." So breathe and enter the stillness.

Today during meditation, open your heart to space.

Over the past few days, you've been working to reduce resistance to thought. Now, open your heart to nothingness. Sometimes when I meditate and my mind becomes totally quiet, I begin to wonder what I'm supposed to be doing or thinking.

And when your mind goes there, let it know that it's okay to rest in space, in nothingness.

See how many thoughts arise because they're actually there and how many arise because you're afraid of what's beyond them.

This entry into nothingness will be so tentative at first. A split second here, another there. As you experience slices of stillness, don't judge them for how frequently or infrequently they come, how short or long they last.

Just notice the thoughts and notice the space between the thought. Accept everything as it is.

It takes time to release fear of the void. Take your time. Open up to the possibility of being safe in space. Free-falling and not needing to control what comes next.

Journal prompts

What is your relationship to space, to nothingness? In what ways do you fill your time to avoid feeling spaciousness? What fears do you have around emptiness? Creating space for our lives creates room for magic.

Day 6: Inner demons and the Wizard of Oz.

An underrated, but necessary skill when it comes to meditation is courage. So many people resist meditation for years, and that resistance is typically fueled by fear. You may have felt trepidation about sitting with yourself every day, but right now, give yourself a big hug because you are showing bravery simply by showing up every day and meditating!

Consider for a moment your relationship with meditation prior to this point. Have you felt afraid of it? What were you afraid of?

Consider also your experiences over the past few days within the framework of any fear or confusion you may have felt prior to this course. How has your relationship to meditation or yourself shifted over the past week? What has been the high of the your experience so far? What about the low?

Taking a moment to congratulate yourself for the work you've already done and recognize any blips of peace or connection you felt will help you continue developing the meditation habit over the next three weeks and beyond.

It's this deepened experience that will help you develop an unshakeable trust within yourself, which in turn will give you courage. The more you trust yourself, the more courageous you'll feel. That's what this journey is ultimately about.

A lot of talk circulates on dispelling fear, but fear will always be present in some capacity. Even today, I still resist sitting with myself sometimes.

Going within and learning to co-exist with and love things we'd rather run from isn't always easy. But, as I hope you've already seen, it's worth it. Finding the courage to go within helps you dissolve any painful feelings inside and opens your heart to peace, joy, connection and expansion.

Develop courage by practicing daily; daily practice keeps you courageous.

When you're lighting the fire of desire for peace within and committing to a daily practice, you're igniting the wick of courage.

Courage keeps your practice burning even when it gets tough. Courage will help you breathe through any discomfort that arises so that you can transmute it into peace and wisdom.

When you feel fear or resistance rise, accept it, don't repress or resist it.

Acknowledge the existence of this feeling, and then summon your inner courage. Think about your previous successes or maybe the vision you set before starting this course, the ideal of your best, most vibrant self.

Imagine how you'll feel after you sit with this feeling or face these inner demons and allow that vision to inspire you to continue. This way you're not fighting, but expanding.

Always remember that nobody feels peaceful all the time.

Even people who seem to have perfect lives all have inner demons they must look in the eye. Remember that most people come to spirituality not because they've had an easy life, but because they encountered suffering and inner turmoil and began this journey to find peace.

It's my intention that these ideas inspire you to remind yourself that no matter what you're feeling, you're never alone. Learning to sit with what is and accept what is, is part of the human condition. The good news is that this journey holds great promise.

In truth, these demons are merely large shadows, projections on the movie screen of your mind. They're like the wizard in The Wizard of Oz, who seemed to be a scary entity, but was actually just a small, old man speaking through a microphone.

The deeper you look into them, the wispier they become. Just as a projector image relies on darkness to remain vivid, the shadows can't survive for long in the light of pure awareness.

Have faith that your own pure light will dissolve whatever discomfort you face. You'll enter the pain, the discomfort or resistance, and as soon as you summon your courage and cultivate curiosity, breathing into this place of discomfort, the demon will start to vanish.

These things inside of us, they're not mean to cause eternal internal pain. They simply exist to call our attention home.

Like a physical wound requires care to heal, so too do our energetic wounds.

They're calling on us to nurture them with love so that our souls can ultimately expand beyond them. In this way, our wounds fuel spiritual growth by requiring us to summon our courage and go within.

Without courage, the spiritual journey stalls. We must cultivate this sense of fearlessness, even if we're scared — the definition of courage is to feel the fear and continue anyway — in order to fully transmute all our inner pain into peace, love, compassion and understanding.

Otherwise, we continue to hide and look outside ourselves for answers. So be brave. Go within. Feel all there is to feel. And know that you are never alone.

Tips for today's meditation

Today, I invite you to notice any fear you feel and then summon your inner courage to help you go deeper.

Journal prompts

In what areas of your life are you courageous? What areas of your life could use more courage?

Day 7: Warmth, fuzziness and meditation.

Welcome to Day 7! You made it through the first week! I'm so very proud of you! You're doing an amazing job. Give yourself a big hug or pat on the back because you deserve it!

In fact, you should start hugging yourself way more, or at the very least, congratulating yourself more. Learning to become your biggest cheerleader is so important.

Yesterday, we talked about courage, but courage without compassion is ice cold. Think about someone crying in grief. Spirituality without compassion would say, "Life is temporary. Don't be sad. Be happy they're no longer suffering." While this is technically true, it lacks compassion and heart.

Compassion is developing the ability to sit with our own discomfort so that we can sit with others. This is why I advise against searching for happiness for happiness' sake. Happiness is the other side of sadness. It's passing. Temporary.

We know deep down that happiness is fleeting. People attached to happiness create walls around their hearts and close themselves off to preserve the high.

Meanwhile, the deep joy that comes from sitting with all that is, is expansive. All-encompassing. Joy doesn't fear pain because true, deep joy arises from intimacy with life itself, all the ups and all the downs.

Cultivating compassion for our own pain so we can move through it is the starting point for boundless joy and freedom. Courage is the backbone for this journey.

When you feel sad or lonely, try not to judge yourself, but just love yourself. Go within and open up to the experience of how you truly feel.

Compassion complements courage because it makes the journey feel better, just as courage gives compassion a needed edge.

Treat yourself with compassion, but always have the courage to keep going deeper. The deeper you go, the more space there is to explore. Our work never ends.

Today, I invite you to hold the energy of compassion in meditation. Feel it for yourself, and then allow it to extend outward. Notice any dark places within this exercise highlights for you.

If you desire, try the Loving Kindness meditation, also known as metta, from the Buddhist tradition.

The mantra is: "May you be happy, may you be at peace, may you be free of suffering."

If you try this meditation, start first with yourself. Repeat the mantra and send loving kindness to yourself. Then, think of a loved one or friend, continuing to repeat the mantra.

Next, move on to a neutral person, perhaps an acquaintance. As you feel ready, envision people with whom you have strained relationships and continue repeating the mantra. You might consciously think of specific people, but if a person comes to mind, then follow your intuition and allow your higher intelligence to guide this healing process.

End by sending this mantra out to the entire world, all living beings. Take your time and feel free to adapt the practice to meet your needs.

The idea behind this Loving Kindness meditation is that we don't need an apology to forgive. We can find peace in our own hearts and let go because it helps us be free.

As a final Week 1 note, you now have a strong foundation for exploring meditation.

It's my hope that the past week began to ignite within you the fire of confidence, the knowing that you can't meditate wrong as long as you show up with the intention to connect.

The next few weeks will feature a mix of practical tools, insights and mindset shifts to help you deepen your practice. Please know that the biggest gift you can give yourself is that of trusting your innate ability to go within, to know that whatever arises is okay.

All our lives, we've been taught not to trust ourselves, to look around us for answers and validation. The journey into yourself is the journey of forgetting about that directive and looking inward instead of outward. There is no greater expert or guru than you.

Tips for today's meditation

Start by setting the intention to feel compassion. It's okay if you have trouble feeling the feeling on demand; simply setting the intention is more than enough.

Next, if you feel called, try the Loving Kindness meditation.

Journal prompts

How has your relationship to meditation or yourself shifted over the past week? What has been the high of the your experience so far? What about the low?

Week 2: Focus and relaxation

This week, you'll learn my no-fail technique for silencing the relentless mind chatter. Peace out, stress and anxiety!

You'll explore ways of shaping your meditation practice to achieve your specific goals so you can create a practice that works for you.

You'll finish this week feeling empowered and confident, no longer worried if you're doing things right.

Day 8: the antidote to anxiety.

Welcome to Day 8 and Week 2! This week is all about focus and relaxation. You'll discover specific techniques for focusing and visualizing, and also learn key mindset shifts to connect to the safety within so you can feel more peaceful. And with that, onwards!

The opposite of relaxation is of course tension, stress and anxiety. Many people meditate as a way to soothe anxiety and fear about what's happening in their lives or the world.

Energetically, anxiety relates to the first chakra, located at the base of the spine. This chakra can represent fears around survival and basic needs like money, work and health. Physically, it's associated with the feet, legs and adrenal glands, which produce cortisol, also known as the stress hormone.

The root chakra also relates to the Earth, which is why one antidote to anxiety is connecting to nature by spending time outside or even doing something as simple as lying on the floor. Get back into your body and breath, and out of your head.

These actions reconnect you to the sense that you are are supported by something far greater than you. Nature reminds us of resilience and life's cyclical nature. This in itself is a powerful antidote for anxiety.

Honoring life's cycles helps us see our problems from a larger perspective. Remembering that day follows night reconnects us to the impermanence of life. Rainbows follow storms, happiness follows sadness, new beginnings follow endings, and life — from a reincarnation perspective, follows death. Our problems don't last forever, and when we stop worrying, we can use that energy to find solutions. This approach deepens your faith in your ability to navigate challenges, which reduces anxiety, but also deepens your faith in the flow of life itself.

When there is a lot of fear around a situation, we can become emotionally attached to our worries. In these times, I offer an unconventional approach: it's helpful to come to peace with the very thing you fear.

This helped me find peace during the coronavirus pandemic. I felt intense anxiety and sat with that emotion in meditation, asking what I was truly afraid of. (Also know that coming to peace with your feelings around a situation is part of accepting the situation itself. By befriending any anxiety you feel, you're starting to move beyond it.)

When you sit with your emotions and quiet your mind, a message will rise up. This message reveals the truth of why you feel the way you feel and also the guidance of how to move beyond it. But you must quiet your mind. A lot of times the mind jumps in with a fast answer, but it's not always the truest answer.

You know the truth because it feels more solid and grounded. It feels peaceful, and it often rises up from deep within your body rather than a more frantic, surface-level thought.

When the quick answers come, thank them for coming and simply ask, "And what else?" It's important to appreciate the answers for rising up because if you judge yourself for not getting 'the right' answer right away, this causes resistance and places you at war with yourself.

While sitting with my emotions in meditation during the pandemic, I realized I most feared dying alone. So I faced that fear. I thought about what that would be like. I thought about myself lying in bed or the hospital, suffering, dying alone. And I realized that it would suck, but I would deal with it like I have dealt with every other difficult experience in my life — moment by moment.

I knew that if I got better, it'd be another difficult experience I survived and learned from, and if I died, it was my time to go. I'd no longer suffer, and perhaps in my next life, I'd apply some of the lessons I've learned from this lifetime and live more joyfully.

These are processes and questions you can use to come to peace with anything. To use times of struggle to dig a little deeper and find your strength.

When you come to peace with your fears, you gain an incredible sense of confidence and inner peace that allows you to move from desire, hope and faith rather than the fear of what you don't want to happen.

Coming to peace with your fears allows you to no longer feel afraid. Coming to peace with the fact you don't have control allows you to find your inner power. This makes you unstoppable.

So if you feel anxious or afraid, sit with it. Accept the emotion first. Then, ask yourself what you're really afraid of and ask your higher self how you can move beyond that fear. You are stronger than you could ever know.

Tips for today's meditation

Connect to any fear or anxiety you're experiencing. Sit with this energy, not judging it or wishing it would go away, but simply noticing it. What does it feel like? What is the quality of its energy? Where does it show up in your body? How does it move? Use your breath to connect to it.

Journal prompts

What are you afraid of? If any of those fears seem surface level, feel free to ask, Why am I afraid of that?

Thinking about those fears, what is the worst-case scenario? Connect to your higher self. If you were in that worst-case scenario right now, what would be the highest and best way to respond? What would you know in that moment to be true that would give you peace?

Connecting back to this moment, how can you show up for your life in the best possible way?

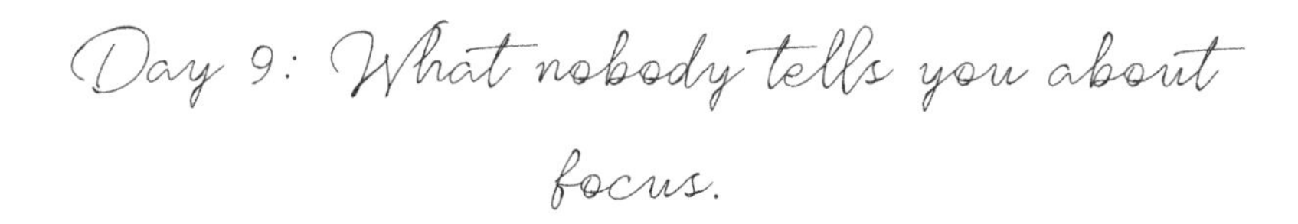
Day 9: What nobody tells you about focus.

Welcome to Day 9! When you meditate, where do you focus? This is a great question. Let's explore.

Focus on one thing

1. The most common meditation instruction is to focus on your breath.

This is a wonderful practice, and if you do this, simply watch the breath enter and leave your body. Notice how it feels sailing past your nostrils and filling up the belly.

Allow yourself to experience the pleasure of your body filling up with beautiful, sacred breath. Ride the breath as you might ride an ocean wave, in and out. Don't worry about breathing a specific way. In fact as your meditation deepens, your breath might become lighter instead of heavier. Simply watch it and breath however feels natural.

Focusing on your breath, especially deep belly breaths, is great if you want to simply relax and release stress. Personally, the ability to quiet my brain enough to watch my breath is a relatively new development.

It took a long time and wasn't the easiest access point — too close to my physical head maybe? — so don't feel bad if you're having difficulty sinking into a breath-centered meditation. Simply try something else.

2. Another wonderful place to focus is your heart.

This is a more feminine way of focus than breath because it helps you get into your body. Both are calming, grounding and centering, but in different ways.

As you probably know by now, this is my favorite area of focus. Focusing on your heart is the best access point if your goal with meditation is to release painful emotions or heal the past. Simply begin at your heart, connect to your energy, and then expand your focus to include the energy throughout your body, as you feel called.

If no emotions are present that day, I focus on my breath. But it took me a couple years of meditating before arriving to days without lingering emotions. This process takes time, although your process will be unique to you.

3. A third place to focus is your belly.

This is a great place to focus if your thoughts start wandering. Instead of resisting your thoughts, simply notice you're thinking and focus on your belly. Notice it expand and contract as your breath enters and leaves your body.

Belly breathing activates the rest and digest response, the parasympathetic nervous system, which is very healing for your body.

Focusing on one specific thing is a wonderful entry point into stillness.

And some meditation teachers stop here, particularly ones rooted more in psychology and less in spirituality.

In my experience, this point of focus is a doorway. It's an access point into true meditation, which is a state of expansive awareness, a unification with all that is.

Once you enter stillness, release the point of focus and enter into this place of expansion. The state of meditation is a union with all that is. Everything else is just a tool to helps us access it.

Expand your awareness to include everything

Focusing on one thing cultivates concentration, which is a useful tool, but is the opposite of meditative awareness. While awareness is expansion, focus and concentration is constriction.

Concentration involves identifying with one thing to the exclusion of all else. If you're concentrated on a task like writing for example, this isn't technically meditating even if your mind is quiet.

Awareness, on the other hand, is a union with everything. Think about how yoga, the actual word, means union. It's a union of mind, body, spirit and the world. When you're in the state of flow with your body and breath, everything melts together as one.

In awareness, we cannot be disturbed because we are one with everything. While focused, we are easily disturbed because we're identified with a single thing, and anything outside of that thing is a distraction. The idea of meditation is to expand and unify as opposed to identify with one thing.

So use a point of focus, like the breath, but use it as a tool to sink into awareness. And once that awareness develops, drop the tool and allow yourself to expand. This is where courage comes in because it can be scary to let go.

If you find yourself overly focused on the breath, clinging to it, you'll know it's time to let go and allow yourself to expand.

Tips for today's meditation

Experiment with different points of focus, maybe the breath, the belly or the heart. What type of focus helps you relax most effectively? How do these various points of focus make you feel?

Journal prompts

Our lives are the sum of what we focus on. What do you find yourself focusing on the most throughout the day? What could you focus on that would give you more peace, joy and happiness? What do you need to know or do to start creating this shift for yourself?

Day 10: Breathing techniques for deep peace.

Welcome to Day 10! Today, we're exploring breath and using it as a tool to sink deeper into meditation.

Yesterday, you learned about focus, and breath was one of the ways to focus. I didn't want you to get too attached to how to breath, so that's why we explored the secret behind focus before exploring the breath itself.

Along the meditative path, your intention and desire to connect to your highest self is the most important thing — much more important than any technique or words of advice from anyone outside of you.

By now you've jumped into the deep end of meditation and swam around on your own. So now, you can learn how to improve your technique and go even deeper.

How should you breathe during meditation?

Unless you're doing specific breath work, known as pranayama, it's fine to breath normally. Ideally, you're always taking deep belly breaths during all your waking hours, with the stomach expanding and contracting as opposed to more shallow breaths focused in the chest.

This maximizes the amount of oxygen, aka prana/life-force energy, delivered to your cells and increases your vitality.

However, as you fall deeper into meditation, often your breath will become shallower and not deeper. This results from the body's sense of relaxation and could also be because the infinite source is sustaining you more than your physical body.

Breathing techniques

In the yoga tradition, breath work is known as pranayama. This practice typically follows a physical practice of asana and precedes seated meditation. Pranayama can also be used on its own or anytime before meditation.

One simple type of breath work is counting the rhythm.

Try this: Inhale for a count of four, hold for four, exhale for six, hold for four. Feel free to change count, but keep your exhale longer than your inhale. Elongating the exhales encourages calm in the body. This is a wonderful practice to try before sleep or anytime you're feeling stressed.

If you do this before meditation, simply breathe for a few minutes and then drop the technique when you feel calm to enter stillness.

You can also simply keep an even breath count, inhaling for four, holding for four and exhaling for four. This is also calming, just less dramatically than the extended exhale.

Another easy breathing tip is to consciously use your exhales. Often when we come to a seated practice, the natural inclination is to inhale first, but it's often nice to reverse that and exhale first. This allows us to let go of all our stresses and worries before receiving on the inhale.

When you exhale, really press the belly button back towards the spine and squeeze all the air completely from your stomach before returning to the inhale.

Nadi shodhana or alternate nostril breathing

This is a powerful breath to activate the parasympathetic nervous system, which calms down the nerves and creates balance.

To begin, lift your right hand to your nose, placing your pointer and middle fingers between your brows in the third eye area. Keep the left hand on your knee.

Gently close your right nostril with your thumb and take a few full inhale and exhale cycles through the left nostril, which is the mellow, passive side of the body.

After a few full breath cycles, pause on the inhale, close the left nostril with your ring finger and exhale out the right nostril. Inhale the right nostril, close that side with the thumb, and then exhale from the left nostril, keeping your breaths long and even.

Inhale from the left nostril, close the left nostril with the ring finger and exhale from the right nostril, making sure to keep the breaths long and slow.

Essentially, you're switching sides each exhale, pausing at the top. Continue this breath for a few minutes, however long feels good for you. It can be nice to breath this way for three minutes and then sit in regular meditation for another five or ten minutes.

Regulate your breathing to regulate your emotions

In yoga it's said that every emotion has a corresponding breath pattern. By regulating the breath, you can regulate your mood to calm anxiety, sit with sadness or find peace in anger. Focusing on specific breath counts is a wonderful way to calm the mind.

Rather than intending to get rid of your emotions, use the breath to create a feeling of stability and safety inside that allows you to feel what you need to feel, or allow yourself to find peace if a few deep breaths were all you needed.

Even if you don't practice pranayama, noticing the belly expand and contract is a wonderful way to bring your awareness back to the body when your mind wanders during meditation. Allow your in and out breaths to remind you that everything comes and everything goes, and everything will be okay.

Tips for today's meditation

Try a counted breath before seated meditation, even if only for a few cycles. Notice the difference it makes for your experience.

If you can remember, try noticing your breath throughout the day. How is it? Shallow? Uneven? Try consciously elongating and deepening your breath for the whole day, even when not seated. Exhale. Let it all go.

Journal prompts

Just like the breath is a mostly invisible rhythm that sustains our lives, so to are the daily habits and rituals that make up your day. What is your relationship to the rhythm of your day or life? Where do you find yourself rushing or resisting? What would it look like if you filled those places of your life with space, attention, intention and love?

Day 11: Mantras for bliss.

Welcome to Day 11! Mantras are wonderful tools to guide the mind into a place of deep relaxation. They're also spiritual super vitamins on their own merit, with specific mantras said to produce specific results, such as cleansing your spirit or karma or removing obstacles in life.

Today you'll learn how to incorporate mantras into your meditation practice. Of course, you can always find guided meditations that include them, but when you have the knowledge to use them on their own, it provides you with greater freedom and ability to customize your practice to fit your needs.

What are mantras?

Mantras are repeated words or phrases. Traditionally, they're Sanskrit, but you can transform anything into a mantra, even "I am pure love," or "I love you."

Two of my favorite mantras are Om Gam Ganapataye Namaha, the mantra of Ganesh that's said to remove all obstacles (which in yoga are said to be in the mind), and Makaral Shivaya Namaha, said to dissolve negative karma.

To access the full benefits of these mantras, it's recommended to repeat them 108 times. You can find You Tube videos featuring 108 repetitions to follow along with. You can also purchase (or make) a mala necklace with 108 beads, which is like a rosary to help you count the recitations.

(As a quick point, many mala necklaces you see are beautiful, made of precious stones, and can cost more than $100. They're beautiful, but you can also buy malas made from basic wood beads for $20 or less. Just so you know that malas don't have to be expensive. If you'd like to deepen your meditation practice, the necklaces are wonderful to have.)

Another one of my favorite mantras is Sa Ta Na Ma.

It's from the Kundalini tradition and means infinity, life, death and rebirth — the cycle of creation. Chanting this mantra is said to synchronize you with the harmony of the universe, break mental addictions and cleanse you spiritually.

Sa Ta Na Ma is a wonderful mantra to use on its own, but to access the power of this meditation, known as Kirtan Kriya in Kundalini yoga, use it in conjunction with the hands: On each syllable, touch the thumb tip to each of the other four fingers, index, middle, ring, and then pinkie. While chanting, try to focus at your third eye, in between the brows.

This specific meditation starts by chanting in a normal voice for 2 minutes, whispering for 2 minutes, chanting silently for 4 minutes, followed by whispering for 2 minutes and ending with chanting out loud for 2 minutes.

You can set your meditation app to notify you when it's time to change.

How to use mantras

Mantras can be repeated 108 times, for several minutes, or even just a few times to bring the mind back to the present moment during meditation or beyond.

The stillness that envelops you after chanting for just a few minutes is miraculous. And even though it feels funny at first, it works! If I'm having a bad day where nothing seems to go well, I'll often do one round of Om Gam Ganapataye Namaha, 108 times, followed by one round of Makaral Shivaya Namaha.

I've experienced dramatic shifts not only in my mood, but also in my life after repeating the mantras. One day in particular, I spent the afternoon chanting — you can imagine how frustrated I was to spend the whole afternoon chanting — and a new opportunity to teach yoga — one I'd been anticipating for months — came to fruition. It could be a coincidence, but you never know.

Your family may think you're slightly loony for chanting, but that's okay. They'll get used to it!

Tips for today's meditation

Select a mantra that works for you and try chanting before meditation. You might choose a Sanskrit one or English affirmation, but try repeating it for 11 minutes or 108 times.

As with all the other tools we use, mantras are just another technique to enter stillness. The idea is not to hold onto the mantra forever, but to use it to quiet the mind and then drop into meditation.

Journal prompts

In addition to helpful mantras, we all have not-so-helpful mantras, things we repeat to ourselves all day long that cause us to war with ourselves and life.

Think of a situation you're unhappy about. What are some of the mantras, or thoughts, you repeat to yourself about this situation or yourself? What would you like to tell yourself instead?

Day 12: Visualizations for healing and relaxation.

Welcome to Day 12! Today we're diving into the world of visualizations. You'll learn a few ready-made ones to explore and receive tools to create your own.

These mental images are so powerful in part because the subconscious mind can't differentiate between what's real and imagined.

As you probably know, the subconscious sabotages us if mired in fear, doubt and old wounds. On the flip side, we hold the power to transform this part of ourselves into a powerful ally with healing visualizations that give it something positive to latch onto. So, let's begin!

Golden light

This is perhaps one of the simplest, nicest visualizations to do. You might visualize golden light emanating from your heart center, third eye, top of your head at the crown chakra or your entire body.

If you're experiencing pain in a specific part of your body, you could send golden light to that area. Pro tip: If I'm talking with someone and the conversation is stressing me out, I envision a ball of protective light surrounding me. It works!

You might visualize the light pulsing, or simply follow it as it moves around your being.

Try this golden light meditation: Breathe in, envisioning your entire body filling up with golden light that enters through the crown chakra at the top of your head. As you exhale, envision darkness, feminine receptive energy, seeping in through your toes and filling up your body. Continue inhaling as golden light fills your body and exhaling as peaceful darkness fills your body.

Nature visualization

If you're having a stressful day, it can be nice to close your eyes and visit someplace peaceful. Envision your favorite place, maybe a beach or forest. You might envision yourself gently rocking on a canoe in the middle of a lake.

If you'd like, you can find nature sounds on YouTube to create the perfect background for your visualization.

Anytime you feel stress rising, this place is always available to you. Even closing your eyes for just a moment and envisioning waves washing up on the shore of a beautiful beach or imagining your feet making soft noises as you pad through a thick forest can dissolve tension and bring you back to center.

I live in the desert and miss the ocean pretty much every day. I often close my eyes and envision my favorite beach when my outside environment stresses me out. This is technically a form of escape, of tuning out and not tuning in, but hey, sometimes we need it.

Chakra-inspired visualizations

Each chakra, which is a center of energy located along the spine, emanates a specific color. Envisioning a colored, glowing ball of light shining from the chakra's physical location can be a wonderful healing practice.

Here is a brief overview of the chakras and the colors you may want to experiment with:

The root, located at the base of the spine, is associated with the feet, legs and skeletal system. This chakra relates to material security, survival and belonging. It's red.

The sacral is located at the sacrum in the lower back. It relates to emotions, creativity, sexuality and pleasure. The color is orange.

The solar plexus, located at the belly, relates to personal will power, confidence and individuality. The color is yellow.

The heart, located at the chest, relates to unconditional love and forgiveness. The color is green.

The throat chakra relates to speaking your truth. It's blue.

The third eye, located between the brows, relates to intuition and wisdom beyond words. The color is indigo.

The crown chakra, at the top of the head, represents our connection to infinity. The color is violet or sometimes white.

To use a chakra meditation, you would focus your attention on the chakra's physical location, imagining the related color shining through. You could also balance the chakras by using this process while moving your awareness from the root to the crown.

To create your own visualization...

Is more art than science. Simply drop in and see what comes up. You could start with one of these suggestions and follow your intuition to see what images arise. You cannot go wrong! As long as it feels good, keep going.

And if something dark comes up, explore it if possible. True healing and transformation come from exploring the dark crevices of our soul, transforming them with awareness into love.

Tips for today's meditation

Try one of these visualizations or another you feel called to, and then enjoy stillness for any amount of time you desire.

Feel free to journal about your experiences.

Journal prompts

We all have visions of our lives inside of our minds. Some of these visions are more helpful than others. What are some of the less helpful visions in your mind, the fears of doom and gloom that keep you stuck and anxious?

What is an inspiring vision of the future you'd like to replace that with? This could be a vision for your whole life, or just one element of life.

If you're not sure what you want in life, check out our Listen to Your Heart guided journal to help you hear the messages of your heart that are guiding you to a life you love.

____

____

____

____

____

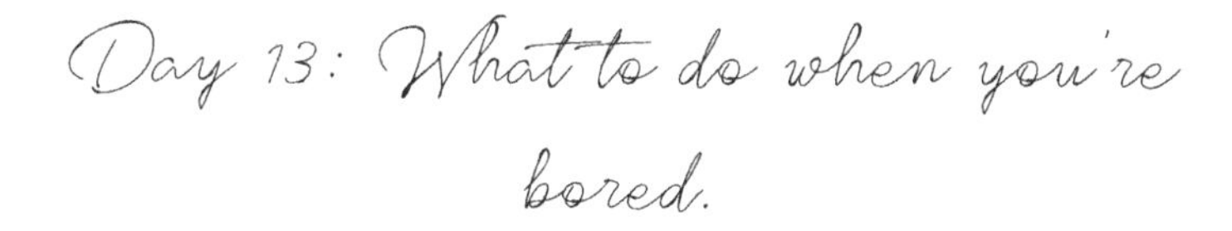
Day 13: What to do when you're bored.

Welcome to Day 13! Boredom is a common experience in meditation. It can actually be a good sign because it means that your thoughts are slowing down to the point that boredom can actually arise.

When you do feel bored, resistance to the practice itself begins to rise. You may wonder what the point is and begin to wonder if you should just skip today's meditation because you have so many other, more interesting things to do. This is when the practice begins, precisely when you no longer want to do it.

How to navigate boredom

The first step, to ensure you continue the practice, is to remind yourself why you want to meditate in the first place. What is the vision of the person who you want to become through meditation? Envision that peaceful, vibrant, centered, grounded person, and allow that vision to inspire your continued practice, despite the discomfort of boredom.

The second step is to put this boredom in perspective. Something I always tell myself is that I can easily spend 10 or 20 minutes (probably more) on social media, reading, or working. And if 20 minutes flies by doing that, then I can instead spend that time sitting here, in meditation, taking my spiritual super vitamin.

The third step is to become curious. Curiosity is the ultimate antidote to boredom. It also removes any resistance you may feel towards it.

Boredom is just another form of resistance, thinking that the present moment should be more exciting than it is. When it develops, consciously tune into your body and breath. Contemplate how miraculous your existence is — your beating heart, your lungs that filter air and feed your body with life-giving oxygen all on their own, the true miracle of this present moment that has you sitting and connecting to your infinite, true nature.

Become fascinated with your existence, the inner world of your feelings, and the depths of the universe within.

As you cultivate this curiosity, you will become more open. This space creates the possibility for true connection. You've already created stillness, boredom signals the stillness. Now your task becomes to appreciate this stillness, to drop in a little deeper and connect more fully.

It might be tempting to switch up your practice a little bit, to do a guided meditation or try a different technique, and that is one possibility. However, consider that this boredom is a great teacher along the path, and that if you learn how to change your relationship to the practice and to boredom itself, then you will have cultivated yet another skill to deepen your experience of life.

Creating variety with different meditation techniques is fine, but it easily becomes another escape. The path of the meditator is to face ourselves — the fire of anger, the blackness of sadness, the sting of regret and the monotony of boredom — with no filter.

If you seek to escape yourself, you may temporarily enjoy success, but you're only delaying the inevitable. Sooner or later you will have to face yourself. The sooner you dive into the boredom, the more quickly you will progress along the spiritual path.

Learn to sit through boredom and you will have dissolved yet another illusion keeping you from the truth of who you really are.

How jam-packed is your life?

If you struggle with boredom in meditation, I also invite you to take a look at your life outside of meditation. Is it crammed full of events, material items and people? Do you need all of those places, people and things, or are they simply taking up space?

Boredom highlights a reluctance to go deeper. There is something within us that resists the stillness, and so we become bored, wishing to be entertained. What are you trying to avoid? Why do you resist space or emptiness? Inside boredom, the greatest revelations, daydreams and new visions lie.

Tips for today's meditation

Notice any boredom that arises. Instead of identifying with it, become curious about it. What does it feel like in your body? What kinds of thoughts and responses does boredom create? How does it influence your perception of self and of meditation?

Journal prompts

Answer the questions related to looking at how jam-packed your life is.

Sometimes it seems like the moment we sit down to meditate, the world becomes so noisy. Dogs bark, trash trucks crash through the neighborhood, trains choo-choo in the distance.

Unless you have the good fortune of living in nature, chances are good that outside noises will distract you from your practice.

Of course we want the perfect meditation, in perfect silence, but this is analogous to how we want the perfect day to unfold in perfect harmony to create a perfect life. Often reality falls short of our cherished ideals.

So what is a meditator to do? The answer is to fold these sounds into your experience. Become interested in the sounds. Release your resistance to them, to the idea that they shouldn't be there, and instead welcome them into your meditation.

A Zen master once posed this question in a book: Is the noise bothering you or are you going out of your way to be bothered by it? (This was a long time ago, and unfortunately I don't remember the book or the teacher.)

That's pretty profound. We tend to build these walls up around our reality and set expectations, even in meditation.

We feel like meditation should be a certain way and establish criteria for what's acceptable and what's not. But how powerful would it be to turn your meditation into a practice where you sit with being annoyed. Where you practice finding stillness amid the very chaos that you'd rather run from.

Of course, this isn't to say that you should go out of your way to meditate in the middle of a playground at recess, but if noises or other unwelcome intrusions arise, invite them into your world instead of building a fence to block them out. It can be interesting to notice not only our reaction to the sounds, but the story that develops in response.

One day I was sitting in meditation when my husband came home, and our dog started barking wildly. As the dog barked, I began to envision my husband entering my meditation space, interrupting me. I noticed the frustration rising at something that hadn't even happened.

I decided to make the noises part of my practice, observing my dog bark while detaching from the meaning that the noise had. I let him bark and allowed myself to release feelings of being responsible for the noise.

My husband came into the house and I listened as he navigated the kitchen, probably placing his gym bag down and pouring a drink or something, but it was so nice to feel like none of this had anything to do with me.

Many women, in particular, feel responsible for caring for everyone in their environment, even when they don't need our care. To sit back and listen to sounds and notice the world go on without you can be the most freeing thing.

Ultimately, he never came into the room. I could have let my frustration consume the practice, obsessing over something that was never going to happen. How often do we do this exact same thing in real life?

Through the practice of sitting with sounds we'd rather not hear in meditation, we develop the ability to cultivate an even stronger sense of calm. Imagine then, the calm that can happen off the meditation cushion when unwelcome experiences arise in life. Everything on the cushion prepares us for real life. That's why it's called a practice!

I feel it necessary to say that of course sometimes sounds do bother me, as do interruptions, but this is something we can all aim for. The ability to develop a sense of peace so deep that nothing outside can disturb us.

May we learn to accept the present moment so fully that nothing disturbs our heartfelt connection to the infinite. When we learn to release resistance and accept what is, we find peace, love and joy.

Tips for today's meditation

Notice any noises while in meditation and notice your response to them. What meaning do these noises hold for you?

Journal prompts

How involved are you in things that don't necessarily require your involvement? What thoughts or emotions are creating that attachment? Where does this attachment come from? If you allowed yourself to let the world work itself out just a little more without you, what would you believe to be true? How would you act?

____

____

____

____

Week 3: Heart & soul

Healing, peace, joy and happiness come from a connection to your body and soul, when the mind quiets and the heart sings.

This week, you'll learn how to tap into your intuition to ask questions of your higher self.

You'll also explore how use meditation as a tool for emotional healing and inner child work. These powerful practices will change your life.

Day 15: Connecting to heart & soul

Welcome to Day 15 and the start of Week 3! This week is all about heart and soul, which is the essence of our spiritual existence and the meat of meditation itself.

Many people come to meditation in an effort to connect more deeply to their true selves, hear their hearts and intuition, and heal emotional wounds. This practice will provide all that for you and more. This week, we'll explore these themes and you'll discover how to activate this healing potential.

The most important thing is to keep meditation pure, to approach the practice with the intention of connection and commitment.

It's fine to want to heal and find answers, those are important gifts of meditation, but they don't come when we demand them. They come when we soften into them.

Everything is available to us when we soften into it. Think of how this translates into the rest of life. When desperately seeking love or work or new opportunities, they don't come. It always seems like when I stop caring and go about my life that things effortlessly fall into place.

The universe doesn't respond well to the energy of desperation. And so we must approach meditation as a place to practice softening into the knowing that everything is already ours, all the answers and all the healing.

It was always yours, so there's nothing to worry about.

This idea of softening pertains especially to tuning into our intuition. When you ask for answers and don't create the space for them to arise, instead filling that space with worrying and fear, there's no room for intuition to arise.

And even if it did, you wouldn't trust the wisdom. You'd doubt it and worry if it was your intuition or something else because you haven't created the receptivity necessary to open up to deeper messages. You're not connected enough to your higher self to choose faith.

Ultimately fear and doubt come from identifying with your smaller self. The antidote is to connect to the universe, your higher self and soul. Be so deeply connected to the higher truth that lower vibrations have no room to exist.

On another level, trusting the universe allows you to trust yourself, and vice versa. We must soften, surrender and release control. This is our journey through life and also through meditation.

When I was younger, I lived on Maui for a short time. It was a very healing experience; my father and sister had died about 10 years earlier, but I had never processed the emotions because I'd spent my life thinking I had to be strong and cold and never hurt.

Maui was so healing in part because it taught me how to let go and soften up to the universe. The island, her mana, or energy, is so healing, but there was a specific practice I did to encourage this process. I'd go in the ocean and body surf the waves, and while each wave carried me to shore, I consciously released tension in my body and practiced relaxing into the wave. It was a practice of letting go.

This is analogous to meditation, which is the practice of relaxing into the universe by relaxing into your breath and body.

An easy way to start this relaxation is by noticing tension in the body, consciously breathing into it and releasing. As the body relaxes, so will the mind.

This is a nice practice to do throughout the day — simply pause for a moment and notice any tension you're carrying. Creating awareness around this tension and simply breathing into it allows you to relax.

Through this relaxation, we open up to healing and hearing answers from deep within. Meditation doesn't create answers that weren't already there. It opens us up to hear what's always been there.

Tips for today's meditation

Practice relaxing, noticing and breathing into tension in different parts of your body. Watch how this practice of noticing and releasing physical tension affects the mind.

Journal prompts

What in your life makes you tense or stressed? How do you respond when you feel this way? What would it look like to soften around this tension? How could you better respond?

____

____

____

____

____

____

Day 16: Hear your intuition.

Yesterday, we discussed the importance of relaxing into meditation, coming to it with the intention to connect, and today you'll learn how to explore your intuition a little more deeply.

Even though today you'll be applying more effort to accessing intuitive messages, I invite you to continue cultivating that relaxed energy of lightness.

What is intuition?

Intuition is knowing beyond knowing. It's beyond words, beyond logic and beyond reasoning. Different people access intuition in different ways. Some may see visions, others may receive thoughts, and still others may feel specific feelings, or any combination.

More on this tomorrow, but emotions are an important part of your intuition. If you repress or reject your feelings, it's likely you're also cut off from your true self, including your wants, needs, dreams and intuition. Inquire within: How true is this for you?

The more you follow your intuition, the louder it becomes.

We all have access to this voice, but mind chatter and unprocessed emotion blocks us from hearing it. These things make us reactive and distrustful, when intuition requires us to respond with intention and trust. Feelings are also an important part of your internal guidance system. Increasing your capacity and willingness to feel emotions will amplify your intuition.

Once you hear your intuition, even the slightest whisper, you must follow it. So often, we ask for messages, but then doubt ourselves when they appear. Don't doubt. Trust.

Meditation increases intuition several ways. First, it stills the mind to create an empty container for the intuitive voice to arise. It acquaints you with the subtleties of your many internal voices — the voice of doubt and fear, and the voice of your higher self.

We spend so much time telling ourselves no — don't do that, don't think that, don't feel that — that it's really no surprise that our intuition dims. Meditation makes you more receptive to all of life, and that includes the flow of your innate wisdom.

Meditation is analogous to cleansing your palate from all the influences of the world, making intuition easier to hear.

It's like if you stop eating sugar for a while and the tastes of fruits and vegetables become much more nuanced and enjoyable.

Energetically, meditation strengthens your third eye and increases the flow of prana, life-force energy, into the crown chakra at the top of the head. As you literally become more full of spirit, the voice of spirit cannot help but make itself known.

How to deepen your intuition

A key element of intuition is to trust it. Your heart's knowing is soft. The voice of doubt tends to crowd out the voice of truth. It takes practice, patience and continued listening to identify intuition.

Over time, your intuition will amplify, but perhaps most importantly, you'll trust yourself more. Intuition is a lightness, an unclenched fist. The more you relax, the more wisdom you'll hear.

As you practice following your heart, you'll learn from how life responds to you and fine-tune this internal compass. That said, if you make a wrong move, it's okay, it's a learning experience. Use the experience to fine-tune your intuitive radar.

In addition to meditating, other simple ways to increase your intuition include:

- Ask your higher self what you'd like to wear each morning. Allow a moment of space and see what outfit comes to mind.
- Ask for help deciding what to eat. Again, take a moment to pause and allow an image of a meal to come to mind.
- Limit time spent watching television and on social media.
- Spend more time in nature.
- Eat more whole foods and fewer processed foods.

How to access higher wisdom during meditation

The simplest way to access your intuition is to simply ask a question. "Please universe/higher self/ God, help me figure out which decision to make." Then, release your request and simply breathe.

If you cling to the request, answers will not come. Instead, relax into knowing that you already have the answer, you simply need to tune into it. The answer may come a few moments later in meditation, or it may arise later during the day. It might arise as an idea, or a sign from the universe, such as hearing about a specific idea, book or author multiple times.

Pay attention and remain fluid! Also know that things change. What's good for you today might not be good tomorrow. Stay open and keep flowing with the changing tides.

Tips for today's meditation

Ask your intuition a question and then release it into silence without expectation. Notice what comes up, either during meditation or later that day. Notice any worldly signs that appear, such as themes you read about that appear more than once, or any thoughts or feelings that arise, especially repetitively.

Notice your response to the signs. How do they make you feel? Do you trust or doubt?

Journal prompts

Journal about your experiences from meditation. What is your relationship to your intuition? What holds you back from following it? What would you believe if you trusted yourself more?

____

____

____

____

____

Day 17: Emotions for healing & intuition.

Welcome to Day 17! Today kicks off a few days of exploring the connection between emotions, meditation and intuition. This topic is big and juicy and my all-time favorite.

Meditating with your emotions will help you release them and connect to your true self. Emotions are what so many people spend their lives running from. Yet embracing them and learning from them will transform your life.

What is the point of emotional pain?

Painful emotions exist to let us know something is off in our lives. All emotions have specific messages.

Sadness is a sign we are out of alignment with who we really are. It can also be a release. Tears contain stress hormones, meaning that sadness is the body's way of washing away things it no longer needs just like a rainstorm clears the air.

Anger comes from feeling powerless. It can be a call to resurrect your boundaries, or signal that you've given your power away to another person. It can also be a protective mechanism to coverup deep hurt.

Anxiety means that you feel afraid. You no longer trust life or that your basic needs will be met, including the need for love. You feel cut off from life's flow and need to return back to your body, to resurrect your connection to the Earth.

There are many more emotions, and we will cover their messages in another Soul Scroll Journal. Know that as you sit with your emotions, they will reveal to you their messages as long as you can separate yourself from the story around the emotion.

It's the repeating of the story, attaching to it and believing it to be the only truth that keeps us stuck in our lives and feelings. Tomorrow we will discuss more how to release emotions. Today is more about reshaping your relationship to how you feel so you can create space for healing.

Because emotions have such important messages, they are an important part of your intuition, the way your soul speaks to you and guides you through life.

Feeling this pain not fun, and that's one reason why so many people resist sitting with the raw pain. Another reason is simply that we're not taught how to feel. We're not taught these emotions have value. Even the name — negative emotions — signals these feelings are bad and unnecessary when that couldn't be further from the truth.

We're all human, we all feel and we will always feel no matter how enlightened we become. That makes developing a good relationship with your emotions of utmost importance. Journaling and meditation are the two best ways to do this. In addition to writing about my feelings, I create space each day in meditation to simply feel and suggest that if you are also highly sensitive or emotional, you do the same.

Have faith that soon as you fully feel your feelings in objective awareness, they immediately begin to dissolve. In this way, you can use your pain as a doorway to connect more deeply to yourself.

Practice the Feeling Awareness meditation available for free at SoulScrollJournals.com/bonuses daily for optimal results.

Other causes of emotional pain include...

Another cause of emotional pain happens when you repress or reject your truth, not saying how you really think and feel.

Every time you choose another's comfort over your authentic but kind self-expression, it literally hurts your soul and leads to a life that feels out of alignment.

These incongruences cause pain, and that's the first signal from your internal guidance system that something is awry.

Emotional pain also naturally results after trauma or difficult life events. Feeling that pain, as opposed to pretending it doesn't exist, is the best way to process and heal, to extract the wisdom from the wound. When you accept your emotions, you're also accepting the life circumstances they represent.

Resisting life circumstances, wishing they were different, is a big reason why it can be hard for people to accept their emotions. Accept life by accepting how you feel.

Healing is a subconscious process, one of feeling and allowing the body's innate intelligence to process pain energy. Our emotional bodies know how to digest emotions just like the stomach knows how to digest food.

This process is the most natural thing in the world. As you process your emotions in awareness through feeling, you automatically download the resulting wisdom. When I say download, I mean allow the universe's wisdom to flow into your conscious awareness.

This process also creates a clear channel for you to receive intuitive messages. The more time you spend in stillness connecting to your energy — the energy that is your soul and emotions — the stronger your intuition will become.

If you sit down to feel and notice nothing but numbness or resistance, sit with the numbness or resistance.

Always begin where you are, never judging yourself for that place. Once you face yourself, there's nothing left to fear.

Tips for today's meditation

Start by connecting to your heart. Explore your body energetically, noticing what you feel and how it feels. Rather than trying to analyze or understand, simply feel. Breathe into the sensations. Try the Feeling Awareness Meditation at SoulScrollJournals.com/bonuses to guide you through this practice.

Journal prompts

What is your relationship to your emotions? How do you respond when you you feel pain? What are some of your coping mechanisms, healthy or unhealthy? What are these feelings trying to tell you?

___

___

___

___

___

Day 18: How to feel your feelings.

So excited for today! I get so excited about feelings because learning how to feel and heal them truly changed my life.

Once you tap into their power, you will get excited about feelings, too.

The most important thing to know about emotional pain is that it's the rain before the rainbow. No matter how much your heart hurts during the storm, the peace and clarity you feel after exploring your inner landscape makes it all worthwhile.

This is the sacred act of connecting with your true self. So let's begin!

Tips for feeling your feelings

First, bring your awareness to your heart center and notice what's there. Sometimes it takes a few (or many) minutes of sitting and breathing, creating space to feel. As you drop deeper into your heart, different sensations or energies will arise. You may feel areas of dense or thick energy, perhaps emotions, perhaps nameless sensations.

Simply notice and breathe into the area. Use your breath like a straw, breathing the emotional energy in to drop deeper into the feeling while also anchoring into the present moment. Sit with yourself, no matter what arises. You might set an intention or ask your higher self to help connect you to your emotions, and then sit and breathe until they arise.

Your emotions may feel heavy or solid at first. As you breathe into the sensations, they'll become bigger and stronger. They also tend to feel more diffuse as you merge with the energy and it surrounds you. It's as if the energy becomes a cloud. Breathe into it. Become it. Notice how the emotion feels in your lungs, in your nose, in your heart space.

Cultivate courage. They're only emotions. There's nothing to fear. They will soon pass.

It's easy sometimes to feel overwhelmed by emotion. Use your breath as an anchor while summoning your internal courage to keep going deeper. It may feel like the emotion will never end, but it will. This is the process of feeling and healing.

If you'd like, explore around your inner world with your awareness as if your awareness were a hand, searching in the dark to make sure you don't walk into a wall. Simply explore, set the intention to move energy around and feel, notice what arises. This can help you tap into emotions on the periphery of your internal world. Again, when sensations arise, breathe into them.

This simple technique is the process of feeling and healing.

Emotions typically come in waves

You may feel through to the end of one wave in a meditation session, or sometimes, particularly if you're just beginning this practice, you might walk away from your meditation with an ache still in your heart.

That's okay. Know that every ounce of emotion you feel with awareness is processed. It's just that many emotions are wedged very deep inside. You may have been repressing emotions for a lifetime. It takes time to clear the backlog. Keep showing up with the intention to feel and heal.

Here's the thing that takes the most practice: As you feel strong emotions in awareness, corresponding thoughts will rise. Set the intention to feel and focus on the feeling while releasing attachment to the thought. Feeling the emotion in awareness means feeling the emotion while releasing identification with the thought.

The thoughts are the stories we tell ourselves. This happened, and I'm doomed, or this person did this horrible thing to me. These are stories, and while they may be true, clinging to the story perpetuates the pain.

The emotion is the root, and as you clear away dead roots through feeling and processing, you clear away the resulting dead trees and branches, aka useless and non-helpful thoughts, creating space for more beautiful flowers to blossom.

After a while, you may get excited about new emotions to feel because it's an opportunity for even deeper healing.

This is the process of literally feeling the wounds of your heart and soul and healing them with pure divine awareness.

It's deep, sacred, powerful work and if you commit to this as a lifelong practice, your entire life will change.

Know that as you embark on this journey, you may at times feel overwhelming emotions that last beyond your meditation session. Have faith in the process.

Create as much space as you need to sit with yourself. You can also tell your higher self that you need a break, and the emotions will fade.

Delaying healing when you need to is 100% okay, it can be a great act of self-compassion to press pause. However, know that you will need to face these emotions eventually. When the time is right, ask your higher self for help to resume the process and begin again, fueled by courage.

Tips for today's meditation

Today, sit with your heart without a guided meditation. Just sit, explore and breathe.

Journal prompts

What was sitting with your emotions in meditation like? What struggles or fears came up? What would help you move beyond them?

Day 19: Meditation and inner child work.

Earlier this week, we talked about entering the pain of internal emotions. However, meditation can be used to go even deeper, to ply the depths of your soul, what's known as the shadow.

The shadow is those parts of ourselves we've disowned, the traits we have, emotions we feel or things we do that we'd rather not be a part of ourselves.

If, for example, you acted in a fit of rage and later said, "That's not me. I wasn't acting like myself," that behavior and those emotions would be the shadow. Because clearly, it was you. An alien didn't invade your body, but something activated a wound deep inside of you that you'd rather not look at or perhaps you don't even know it's there.

Our task on the spiritual journey is not to judge ourselves when we act in ways we dislike, but to love ourselves and seek to understand.

Shadow wounds often develop in childhood, or are carried on from past lives, and we can spend the rest of our lives creating a reality around the perceptions these wounds created. Feeling and healing our pain in awareness provides the opportunity to create a life reflecting our biggest hopes and dreams rather than our fears and coping mechanisms.

An ideal of ongoing meditation is to become so free of flawed perception — or at least aware of it — that nothing influences us except for our highest, truest self.

Healing the shadow is a big topic, but today, I invite you to explore an inner child healing meditation/visualization.

Inner child visualization

This is a more specific spiritual healing technique, but it can be used any time you feel that unhealed emotional wounds are affecting your present life.

Connect to a situation causing stress or suffering. As you connect to how this situation makes you feel, allow that emotion to lead you to an image or memory. You can also try asking, "Please show me what needs to be healed."

A memory of the younger you will likely appear. It may seem random, but have faith — no memory is random. Emotions and memories are closely linked, and if a memory comes up for you, it means healing is available. If nothing comes up, keep holding space while releasing the pressure. Set the intention to create a feeling of safety within.

If you feel afraid or don't want to do this work for some reason, a memory won't come up. If this is the case, you might journal on reasons why you may be afraid and how you can see them differently. You could also simply sit with the fear or resistance that arises.

If a memory does come up, hold this image in your mind's eye while focusing on your breath. Explore the situation energetically and flow with it.

There are two scenarios that typically unfold: In the first, your younger self needs to hear from you, your present self. You might tell your younger self that she didn't deserve to be treated this way and offer information or advice that would help your younger self process the life circumstance.

For instance, if your younger self was abandoned by a parent, you might say, "You are worthy of love and protection, and it's not your fault that mom or dad abandoned you. They have their own issues, and you deserve much, much better."

The second scenario is that your younger self has information to give you. This can't be forced, and you will know if this younger self has information to provide.

I did this once, not to myself as a child, but to myself of a few years ago, just before I made a concerted effort to change my life. My old self told me how proud of me she was and told me that she did the best she could, given the tools she had to work with.

Allow a conversation to flow naturally, back and forth. If you'd like to explore this process deeper, head to SoulScrollJournals.com and check out our advanced shadow work video training. There's also a shorter, free version at SoulScrollJournals.com/bonuses.

Ideally, at the end you will feel an integration, with your younger self and present day self merging together energetically to continue walking on this path as one, hand in hand, side by side.

This meditation of course isn't something you would use every day, but can be a powerful technique to have in your toolbox. Use it whenever you feel consumed by the past or feel trapped in a situation and aren't sure how to break through.

Tips for today's meditation

Try an inner child healing based on the guidance from today's reading.

Journal prompts

Write about your experiences from the healing experience. If you feel called, write a letter to your younger self.

Day 20: Higher self vs. lower self.

Welcome to Day 20! Perhaps along your journey of spiritual development and meditation, you've noticed dueling voices, those of the higher self and the lower self.

It can seem like these two voices are at war, an angel on one shoulder and a devil on the other. It takes time to listen and learn which voice is real, to sort out the dueling voices and feel an inner sense of order rise once again.

Know that this discomfort is an important part of your journey. Embrace the struggle and learn from it. Dive in and actively explore these inner voices to learn from them. What do they each wish to say?

Along the way, you may experience confusion like:

- Is the voice of fear actually fear or is it your intuition, giving you an important sign?
- Is the voice telling you to pick up and leave the voice of your higher self, urging you to risk it all for your own freedom? Or is it the voice of your lower self, trying to ruin your life with resistance?

These voices always exist within us, and as meditation increases your awareness, so does the realization that they are, in fact, two separate voices.

Look carefully, and you'll see that they feel different, no matter how confusing your efforts may be to differentiate.

The rationale for the loving voice will feel loving, even if it's not easy. The rationale behind the voice of fear and resistance, on the other hand, will try to win at another's expense. It will tell you to make a move because you're not good enough, or don't deserve good things. It will play scarcity, and tell you there's not enough time. It will violate your deeper core values for the rush of instant gratification or to escape something difficult.

Perhaps this is why over time the voices become easier to differentiate. Because as you tune into your goodness, you understand that any voice telling you otherwise is lying. Any voice playing on your fears is lying. As you know who you are more intimately, the voice of your true desires and needs becomes more obvious. As you understand these dueling forces within, the voice of your higher self and intuition gets louder and easier to hear.

The lower self will scream; it's insistent and demanding. It's so sure of itself, yet its words don't feel right — how is this possible?

Sometimes, the loudest, most confident voice is not the voice of intuition at all. Sometimes the voice of intuition is the quiet voice that whispers and waits until after you completely break down to make itself known. After the breakdown comes quiet, the rainbow after the storm. When you're humble enough to listen, the intuition speaks.

As meditation makes you increasingly humble and receptive, your intuition will become louder and easier to hear.

(Quick note: Humility is not about being weak or powerless. It's simply understanding that you don't know everything and deferring to the wisdom of the universe.)

Just know, that if you're not sure, you don't have to act right away. Don't make moves when angry or upset. Understand that thoughts drunk on emotions rarely reflect the highest good. Wait until calm. Peaceful thoughts are typically loving thoughts.

And this is where meditation's gift of non-reactivity comes in. Most things in life are not that urgent. They can wait. Give yourself time to wait and listen to the voices, hear the rationale behind each.

The more intimately you know your higher self and smaller self, the more you'll be able to differentiate between their voices. The better you know your small self, the more you know how it tries to seduce you, which fears it plays. Become aware of the small-self voice and consciously choose to not believe it.

Sometimes, I simply laugh at my lower self — its contribution is truly comical. If this doesn't work for you, you might thank the voice of the small self for its input, and then affirm that its thoughts don't reflect the true you.

Align with your highest self through meditation. Know that every second you spend illuminating your higher self and choosing against your lower self is a small tear in the skin of smallness you're shedding.

The process grows easier over time, but it's a life-long journey of understanding all sides of you, bathing your entire being in the light of pure awareness, and becoming conscious about which voices you choose to believe. If you make a mistake, allow that mistake to teach you. Don't judge yourself, we're all learning how to go home.

Quick tip: Ask your highest self for help

Our highest self is always there waiting to offer assistance, but it typically needs an invitation. Simply ask for help seeing a situation differently, and insights always come.

Tips for today's meditation

Notice the quality of energy underneath your thoughts. Is it fear or is it truth? Throughout the day, become aware of the thoughts running through your mind. Which come from the higher self and which from the lower?

Journal prompts

Consider a situation you've been grappling with. What are the dueling voices when it comes to this situation? What does your lower self say? What does your higher self say? How does each voice feel? Get to know these voices so you can tell the difference in the future.

Day 21: Laughing & meditation.

Although the spiritual journey can feel like a heavy, serious endeavor, the gift of increased presence ultimately allows us to experience more joy and an enhanced lightness of being.

It may not feel that way while breathing through the pain of sadness, anger or resistance, but the gift of feeling these emotions in awareness is the ability to transcend them, to go beyond them. Otherwise, we hold on to the energy, it never fully processes, and shards of it impact our lives beneath conscious perception.

While meditation is not the most fun activity to do, it makes life more joyful.

It gives us the ability to travel through the world unencumbered, less burdened by our problems. It gives us a powerful technique, some call it a spiritual technology, for processing the pieces of life that would normally hold us down, possibly forever.

Our trials were never meant to consume us, only to teach us and help us expand beyond them. Meditation is the tool through which we allow ourselves to absorb the lessons, heal the pain and then move into lightness.

To clarify, I'm not saying that those who meditate will find a sea of uninterrupted happiness. That is simply not the nature of life. What I am saying is that meditation allows us to enjoy the richness of the highs and lows. It allows us to feel more — as we more deeply feel our pain, we open up to a greater experience of joy.

In fact, you might say that meditation helps you feel more joy by helping you give yourself permission to feel it.

Several personal development experts have written about the idea that we close ourselves off to joy because we fear it. (If you're interested in reading more, Brene Brown writes about this in *Daring Greatly* and Gay Hendricks explores it in *The Big Leap*.)

Meditation in many ways is a practice of sitting with our fear because it's our fear of the unknown that closes us off to life's most wonderful experiences. As you deepen your courage through showing up again and again, sitting with yourself no matter what, you're increasing your capacity to experience unadulterated joy.

With the increased mindfulness you enjoy, you reduce the likelihood that you'll subconsciously block yourself from greater levels of happiness and abundance through a fight, drama, or other hardship that starts from habit, limiting belief or self-sabotage.

Finding joy in meditation

Bringing laughter into your meditation practice is an unusual way to experience greater levity and joy. Some people practice laughing yoga, and there are laughing meditations, too. Today, I invite you to give laughing meditation a try if that resonates with you.

Tips for today's meditation

Spend 30 seconds or a minute laughing before meditation. It will feel funny at first, perhaps the whole time, but give it a try for as long as feels comfortable for you. Release. Begin deep in the belly and allow the sound, even if it's forced, to reverberate throughout your being.

You will feel such a shift in your energy, even if you just manage a chuckle or two.

Journal prompts

What areas in life are you taking too seriously? What thoughts, fears or unhealed past experiences contribute to this heaviness? What would it look like to bring a greater sense of lightness and ease to life? What affirmations or attitudes would support this shift?

Week 4: Presence and infinity

This week will set you up for forever success. You'll learn the essential steps to making this practice your own, instead of feeling stuck with habits that don't serve you. (Nothing kills a sparkly new habit more than not enjoying it.)

You'll learn critical mindset shifts, tips for re-igniting any stalled momentum, and ways of transforming every moment into an opportunity for connection.

Day 22: How to overcome resistance.

Welcome to Day 22 and the start of Week 4, our final week together! I hope you've enjoyed this journal, and that it's helped you find a sense of peace and safety within. Thank you so much for being here!

Last week, we dove deep into the heart of the practice, and this week we'll zoom out and talk about the practice itself, addressing common obstacles and mindset shifts to help you cultivate meditation as a companion on your lifelong spiritual journey.

One of the biggest hurdles that meditators face when maintaining the habit is resistance to the practice. As someone who has been meditating regularly for a couple years, I will say that resistance still arises.

Resistance to meditation tends to arise precisely when you need it the most. When life feels difficult and everything seems out of whack, when you know you should go within, sometimes those are the moments of fiercest resistance.

Have you ever been too tired to sleep? Too dirty to feel like showering? To thirsty to drink? Sometimes that's how meditation is, too. You're too filled with depression or anxiety or anger to practice. The last thing you want to do is sit with yourself even though it's exactly what you need.

Over time, this relationship may shift. You may start to crave stillness as a way to soothe uncomfortable feelings. However these moments of needing to meditate and not wanting to are very real. So what do you do?

How to handle resistance to meditation

1. Become aware of your resistance.

It's easy when you're resisting to find excuses that make perfect logical sense or appeal to your emotional self. You're anxious, but 'don't have time.' You're sad, but 'just don't feel like it.'

You tell yourself you'll meditate but find yourself wasting time scrolling on social media or eating your feelings.

Rather than fall into these distractions, notice yourself doing it. And label it. Resistance.

2. Imagine how good you will feel after meditating.

We're always ultimately doing what we really want to do. Even when we're doing bad, destructive things and a part of us wants to stop, there's a part of us that wants to continue doing the bad thing otherwise we wouldn't do it.

Sometimes it's important to explore that emotional connection to self-sabotage, but for today, consider this useful tool: Imagine having already meditated and notice how good you feel.

Connecting to this vision of how good you will feel after making a positive choice can help you escape any self-destructive spirals through the positive habit of meditation.

3. Rationalize the time spent.

One of the most common ways to resist the practice is feeling like you don't have the time. When we get busy, it's easy to let a practice fall off, but busy, stressful times are when we need meditation the most.

I like to remind myself that taking 10 minutes to meditate won't substantially reduce how much I get done in a day. If anything, taking time to meditate means I'll get more done because I'll be more focused and relaxed, even though in the moment that can feel untrue.

Another possibility is considering how much time you spend on social media, checking email, worrying, or however else you tend to spend aimless time. Ten minutes on your phone goes by in a flash! Yet 10 minutes in stillness can seem like eternity. Choose eternity. It will make you feel better. It will help you feel like you have more time.

4. Allow yourself a short practice.

As your practice deepens, you will naturally seek out longer times spent in meditation. This is wonderful, but it can also backfire because then you might feel like a failure for skipping your usual 20-minute session.

One way I maintain my practice during hectic times is by allowing the length to fluctuate. Before sitting each day, I ask myself how long I want to devote to the practice.

Sometimes that's five minutes and other times it's 20. Even five minutes is a wonderful way to maintain the habit. Life is not constant. Allow your meditation practice to fluctuate and meet the needs of your life instead of being a slave to the practice.

As your practice develops, your priorities might shift and you may decide to lengthen your sessions. Also, when you feel sad or are going through a rough time, you might want to increase the number or length of your sessions.

But don't force that decision. Allow your practice to evolve on its own, always connecting to your heart and making decisions that best serve where you are in life.

Quick note

This week won't feature tips for each day's practice. This is a time of transition and integration, of removing the training wheels and allowing yourself to integrate the lessons you've learned as you feel called to use them.

Enjoy the guided meditation at SoulScrollJournals.com/bonuses or enter stillness on your own. Begin to own your practice, making it unique to you.

Journal prompts

What are you resisting the most in your life right now? This could be a change you know you need to make, an overall situation or something else that comes to mind. What is the story you tell yourself around this think you're resisting? What fears are underneath that story? What do you need to know or do to move to the other side? How can you expand so you become bigger than your problems?

____

____

____

____

____

____

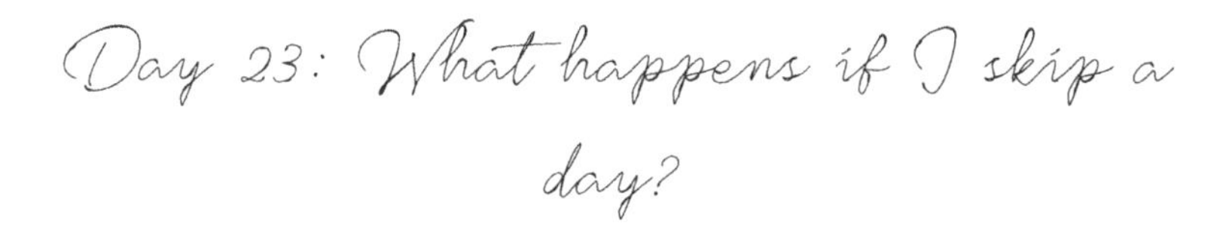

Day 23: What happens if I skip a day?

Welcome to Day 23! Yesterday, we talked about overcoming resistance to the practice, but what happens when you skip a day?

It happens! Life gets busy and then you're too tired to practice, but what about skipping a day intentionally? Deciding in the morning that you don't feel like meditating today.

You know what? It's okay sometimes. The important thing is to learn from it.

The truth is, I'm so nervous to write this. It doesn't seem like a position someone like me should take. But if I'm honest, lapses have appeared in my own practice. Sometimes I get busy, other times I get sick and just want to lay on the couch and do nothing.

Would I be further along in my spiritual journey if I had diligently meditated for 30 minutes every day instead of watching The Kardashians on those days when I didn't feel good?

Probably. But I did what felt right at the time. There is no right or wrong, just show up the best way you can.

We're all human. We all fall off from our habits.

It happens. The important thing is to not judge yourself, but to continue showing up in the best way you know how.

If you skip a day, try not to make it two days. If you skip two days, try not to make it a week.

You might be tempted to give up on the habit all together, but it's better to skip a few days and return to the practice rather than abandon it all together. It's like when people "give up" on their

New Year's resolutions. There really is no giving up or failing because every day is a new chance to begin again.

Sometimes giving up can be helpful. It illuminates how much the practice influences your life, how much peace it gives you.

Notice the suffering that ensues when you stop practicing and allow that to affirm your commitment to the practice. The practice, both in meditation and in life, always returns to the foundation of courage and compassion.

Know yourself. If you allow yourself to skip meditation every single time you simply don't feel like it, you won't reap the benefits of the practice.

If you're too soft on yourself, you will never progress spiritually and experience the peace and joy you crave. But if you're too hard on yourself, meditation easily becomes a source of tension, and not relaxation.

Find the balance, always working to accommodate your life situation and fluctuating needs.

Your commitment to the practice itself will ebb and flow. Sometimes you'll have to dig deep within to find the discipline to sit and breathe, other times you'll be so in love with the stillness that your cushion will call your name, seducing you throughout the day with promises of peace.

Also keep in mind there's more to mindfulness than seated meditation practice.

Bring the essence of mindfulness into all that you do — awareness while eating, while drinking a cup of tea, noticing the flavors and giving gratitude.

Slow down in conversation, really listen and allow others the space to be heard. Making life more mindful is a gift of meditation, and you can be more intentional about that even if you skip a day.

The important thing is to think long term and not give up on yourself. If you skipped exercising for a week, it's best to get back to the gym. It's okay. You probably won't win a bikini contest, but if you're in the game to feel good, then it's okay.

Same with meditation. You won't win any awards for the most enlightened being, but that's not what this is about. The most important thing is feeling at peace and loving yourself along the way.

Maybe this isn't the hard line that a book like this should provide, but I'm all about being real and practical. And most of us are going to skip a day of meditation. It's okay.

Just make sure to return.

Journal prompts

What is your relationship to quitting things? If you quit often, why is that? What are you committed to in life, or what do you want to be committed to? What needs to change in your thoughts, actions or how you see yourself to become a person who sees things through in a more significant way?

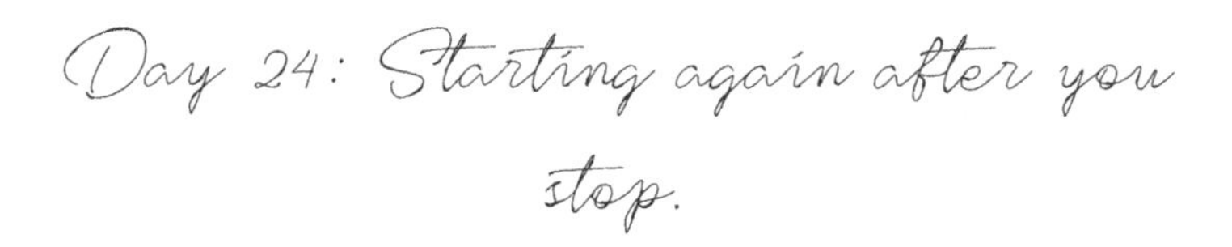

Yesterday, we talked about skipping days of meditation. Yes, it will happen, and no, it's not the end of the world.

But that leaves a pressing question: If you happen to fall off the wagon, how do you return? Let's explore today.

Note that you can use these tips to resume anything after you've quit. Taking a break isn't quitting. Giving up the intention of starting again, is.

How to return to the practice after you stop

1. Notice the changes in your personality.

Typically if you skip maybe one day, but definitely several days, you will start to feel different. Less clear, less calm, more reactive and emotional.

To notice these changes without judgment and then have the awareness to realize they're resulting from not meditating would actually be a great sign. It would show that your awareness is growing. So simply make that connection, and notice how it feels to not feel good.

Try to love yourself and not judge yourself, and allow the desire to feel good inspire your return to the practice. Allow these unpleasant changes to affirm the importance of meditation. Return to the practice without self-judgment.

The key to maintaining a life-long practice is to allow the practice to inspire you. Come to it with love and devotion, not a sense of obligation. This will bring a sense of lightness to the time you spend seated, transforming it into the safe, nurturing place it's designed to be.

2. Do a personal challenge and prioritize meditation above all else.

Pick a length of time, whether that's one week or a full 30 days and make reigniting your meditation practice your top priority.

Often, when I'm not meditating, everything else falls off too, like healthy eating and exercise. I've found that if I simply focus on meditating again, everything else falls into place.

If you want support with creating a new habit, check out our Play with the Day yearly goal journal, which has a habit tracker along with monthly goal and intention setting pages.

3. Allow yourself to start small.

Maybe, when you stopped meditating, you were up to 20-minute sessions. Now that you've dropped off for a few days or longer, the thought of sitting in silence for 20 minutes fills your heart with dread.

So sit for five minutes! Start at the beginning, be where you are. The important thing is that you start.

4. Practice in the morning.

Yes, I've encouraged you to find a time that works for you, but it's no secret that meditating first thing in the morning ensures you actually practice.

If you're having trouble practicing daily, practice first thing in the morning. If your priority is to meditate and feel more peaceful, then you can definitely find the time.

5. Identify time black holes.

We'll go into this more during the final two integration days, but start thinking about where you mis-use time — time that could be spent in meditation.

Do you have too many responsibilities at work or home? Could you delegate or outsource? Do you watch a lot of television? Spend a lot of time on social media? Worry a lot? (Worrying actually takes a lot of time. I've counted. :))

Also consider simple shifts like showering in the evening instead of the morning to free time for practice. Simple changes to shave off a few minutes of your morning routine could help you find that extra time to meditate.

Journal prompts

What have been the positive impacts of meditation and mindfulness you've experienced over the past few weeks? How do you feel differently within yourself and about yourself? Have you noticed any other shifts in your life or relationships?

____

____

____

____

____

____

How do you maintain your meditation practice when life overflows with sweetness? It could be tempting to place your practice to the side, but the biggest benefits develop from consistency.

People often look to spirituality in times of need. You feel stressed out, someone died, you hate your job, your life, and you crave connection to something bigger than you. You long for the sense of meaning spirituality offers.

But then lightness comes. Life is grand. You get a promotion, move to a beautiful new house, fall in love — for the first time or all over again. Sitting down to meditate feels like a buzz kill. You want to revel in the highness of life!

Please do enjoy, but also please continue to meditate. The gift of meditation during life's sad times is that it helps us see everything as temporary. It roots us down in the deepest expression of our true selves and the universe itself, the part of us that is unchanging.

Sadness is a gift because it sends us searching. We want this pain to mean something, or at least to feel less of it. So we seek the eternal that allows us to identify with our inner divinity.

But then bliss comes, and this is what you've been searching for! Now, the danger is high. You want to attach to this happiness, believe it's finally arrived, that high feeling that will never end. You wonder if you've found the key to unlock eternal happiness.

Know that it won't last. Enjoy it, don't squash it from fear or feeling like you don't deserve it — you absolutely do. But this happiness is simply the other side of sadness. Both are temporary states of being lying along different points of the spectrum within our infinite universe.

While it may seem like the biggest buzzkill in the world to enter the stillness of meditation while feeling happy, it's also the most important thing in the world.

Entering the stillness on happy days will ground you. It will help you take a little happiness into your sadness and a little sadness into your happiness, not to ruin it, but to keep you compassionate and rooted.

This way, when happiness leaves, you won't be deflated. In truth, most days for most of us are not happy or sad, but in between, perhaps punctuated by high notes and low. The more you connect to peace, the more you can live in the middle of the extremes.

For many years, my life was marked by high highs and low lows. Every time a period of happiness came, I thought it would last forever. But it never did and the darkness that came after consumed me. Doctors offered diagnoses, but deep in my heart, I always trusted in my own ability to heal, to find peace.

The gift of meditation is that it allows us to feel our feelings in their fullness and connect to the peace beneath, even healing those things blocking us from that peace. Meditation develops the witness part of you that watches your happiness as it watches your sadness. The witness reminds you to embrace whatever you're feeling and reminds you the only constant is change.

Making sure to practice when happy or sad will deepen your relationship with the practice. As your commitment to meditation deepens, so does your commitment to yourself, to be nice to yourself, to be present to yourself, to show up for yourself. As your bond with the practice deepens, so will your bond with yourself. In this way, through meditation, you truly become your own best friend.

Journal prompts

What is your relationship to the highs and lows in life? Do you attach to them, thinking they'll last forever, or perhaps blame yourself for life's inevitable twists and turns? How can you see that differently? In what ways do you unnecessarily hold on to suffering? In what ways do you block joy, or perhaps feel afraid of it?

Day 26: No effort is ever wasted.

Along the spiritual journey of highs and lows, happy and sad, aware responses and unaware reactions, you may sometimes wonder if you're progressing.

It's easy sometimes to feel like you're not, to feel like an angry outburst or day spent crying means you're failing. Maybe you feel like you've backtracked, like nothing is happening, or worse — like the practice isn't working *for you.*

Maybe you've abandoned the practice for a few days or weeks, and you worry if all the progress has washed away, like a sand castle at high tide. Were all those hours for nothing? Do you need to start all over?The answer is a wonderful, resounding no.

No effort along the spiritual path is ever wasted.

Every ounce of illumination has forever changed your heart and imprinted itself in your soul. Sometimes the shifts, the changes are nearly invisible. Progress can be so slow that you don't see it happening.

Sometimes you may feel like you're backtracking, but in truth are examining old patterns from a new or deeper level. I've often felt like I was backtracking in life, but would then read something I wrote from an earlier time and realized my understanding had been deepening the entire time.

We create our lives from our existing level of consciousness, and when we fall into troublesome patterns, it's not that the underlying problem within our consciousness wasn't there. It always was, but hidden. In this way, new problems or even old patterns revealing themselves in new ways can be signs of progress.

They indicate issues in our consciousness that have now been revealed and are ready to be healed. They always existed; they're simply becoming more obvious now. Although the results aren't always apparent, they're always there.

Then the breakthroughs come. Maybe someone yells at you and all you do is notice your breath and think about how much pain the person screaming must be in to act that way.

Maybe you feel stressed and instead of powering through, intensifying tension, you take a minute to breathe and remember that everything will work out, that there's time for everything that matters.

These moments are like cherries on the sundae — that extra special juiciness of recognition that punctuates all those hours spent sitting and breathing.

And then, one day, the opposite will happen. Someone yells at you and you lose it, yelling right back. Someone cuts you off in traffic and you shake a fist. Your loved one leaves a mess in the kitchen, and you complain about how careless and lazy they are. A stupid social media fight steals your peace.

You'll wonder: Am I worthy as a spiritual being? Have I really made any progress? Why do I still think these thoughts and feel these feelings? When will they go away?

Please know that all the time you spent seated on your meditation cushion counts for something. It adds up cumulatively over time, even when shifts aren't apparent and even if you fall out of the habit for a little while.

Even if your time spent in actual meditation doesn't seem more peaceful or Buddha-like, the rest of your life will shift. It will feel better.

And even during those times when it doesn't feel better, you're still changing, evolving. Have faith and keep up with the practice.

The journey is cyclical, and not linear. You may be called to process things in new, deeper ways at various points along the journey. Returning to a topic you thought was long gone is no indication of backtracking, but instead a deeper processing and returning to truth.

Every drop of awareness cultivated brings more light to your life.

A lot of times when people start out on the spiritual journey, they believe this path guarantees good fortune. Some see meditation or yoga as a way to get rid of sadness or anger or win the affections of the universe so only good things happen.

Meditation offers greater peace as a byproduct, but it's not a bypass to suffering. Nor does it remove what makes you human. It's instead an opportunity to sit with those things without judgment. To become aware of them and less reactive.

To sit with the pain until it becomes peace. To sit with the fear until you remember your faith. To sit with the chaos until things make sense — or to find a way to be okay during those times in your life or in the world when nothing does make sense or feel okay.

When I first started meditating and applying myself deeply to the practice, I felt so much peace. I thought I had arrived somewhere. And then a bout of sadness came, and it made me feel bad about myself, like I was a bad spiritual person because I wasn't grateful or joyous enough to prevent this pain.

And then I read a Buddhism essay and the writer discussed how a good mark of growth isn't necessarily how few painful feelings arise, but how quickly you release the stories around those feelings. To release the self-talk of unworthiness or wrong belief that this will last forever. In essence, to separate the thought from the feeling and notice each deeply without identifying with it. Instead, identify with your eternal, unchanging heart.

So, know that you will sometimes feel like you're going backwards, but in truth, no effort is ever wasted.

Journal prompts

How do you react or respond when you lose patience or feel like things are taking too long? If you cultivated more patience in your life, what would that look like? What would change?

Day 27: Where are the results?

At the beginning of meditation, many people have exciting spiritual experiences. You might see mystical lights or feel new energy percolating in your body or experience the universe itself in strange and fascinating ways.

You may have soul-stirring epiphanies, making meditation feel like a grand adventure that will forever enchant you.

Or if this doesn't happen, you may wonder what you're doing wrong. Perhaps you were expecting...something. Where is your endless peace? Why do you still feel like your mind is chattering non-stop? When will this work?

The answer to this is always the same. It's to keep sitting, drop your expectations and continue accepting your experience, no matter what happens.

This journey is about trusting the process. It's about showing up for yourself, and knowing that sometimes you must water seeds for a long time before they sprout. Have patience and commit to yourself for life so you may live the best life possible.

Sometimes people ask — for how long or how much do you have to practice to see results?

Meditation is deeper than that. It's not a direct exchange, but a relationship with yourself and the universe that deepens and changes over time.

Meditation isn't necessarily about "getting" something. It's about spending time connecting with the source of all that is — including you — and allowing that source to direct your life.

It's not a diet, where you can sit in stillness for a week and change your life like many people might try to eat healthy for a week and lose five pounds. This is a lifestyle, not a 30-day cleanse.

The potential alchemy of meditation — to transform everything you resist and fear into peace and fuel for the journey ahead — is what attracts people to the practice.

But this kind of magic isn't an easy fix. It takes dedication and commitment. Big rewards come with big commitments! And in fact, demanding results from your practice will likely slow you down or even set you up for failure. If you're not seeing results, you might quit, when the true rewards are in the journey.

In the physical practice of yoga, sure you might achieve backbends over time, but the true gifts are feeling your body move, shake and stretch, the peace that fills you up after practice, the harmony that comes from an hour spent measuring time in breaths, not minutes.

Meditation is similar, however there are no handstands to achieve, no before and after pictures.

Instead, meditation is a process of opening your heart to yourself. Of chipping away at all the defenses you've built inside of yourself that prevent you from dropping into the present moment without pretense.

Looking for results separates you from the present moment when this whole process is about dropping into it.

It's my hope that over the past month of meditating daily or almost daily, you've seen small shifts. In truth, although your time on the cushion may not seem to change much, over time you will definitely notice a change off the cushion.

The magic happens when something that normally would have driven you mad or knocked you off your center for days hardly seems to bother you. Or, instead of flipping out immediately, something inside of you pulls you back to your breath.

One day I remember driving to the grocery store and randomly began noticing my breath. For me, that was one of those magical moments. Like, ohmygosh I'm noticing my breath outside of meditation!

But even if you're not noticing these things yet, keep the faith. Keep practicing and you will be rewarded.

For meditation to be magical, make it a part of your life.

Regardless of how many years you've been practicing or what experiences you've had along the way, eventually, the practice settles into a routine.

Meditation will sometimes be magical, and your relationship with it hot and heavy, and then, because life is cyclical, the intensity will fade.

You'll sit and breathe in the morning or whenever you practice, and then get up and go on with your day. Sometimes your mind will chatter the entire time and others, you'll drop into deep stillness.

Whatever is, is perfect.

The important thing is to keep showing up. There's a reason why meditation is a habit, like brushing your teeth.

If you stop brushing your teeth, you'll soon experience the grossness of tartar and cavities. If you stop meditating, you'll soon experience the grime of chaos muddying up your heart, mind and intuition. You'll feel icky, disconnected and unclear.

Those feelings will signal you to begin again. Reconnect with yourself and feel the joyous rush of coming home to your heart — the only home you truly need.

So if there's anything to resist, resist the urge to measure progress. Let repetition be your effort, keep showing up, and all will be revealed.

Journal prompts

Have you noticed any shifts over the past month? How has your practice compared to your expectations? Are there any ways it would feel helpful to shift your expectations in meditation or any other area of life?

Day 28: Discipline, devotion and gratitude.

Welcome to the end of Week 4! I hope the topics this week helped you deepen your relationship with the practice and encouraged you to own your place on the path, wherever that may be.

We have just a few days left together, and we're going to make the most of them. Now onto today's topic of discipline, devotion and gratitude.

To some, discipline sounds like a dirty word. But all great things have behind them the effort of showing up again and again, even when you don't want to. We must find reasons to continue even when it gets difficult.

In meditation, difficulties can arise in the form of boredom, emotional pain or numbness, overwhelm, or just general exhaustion from the seeker's path.

While I believe discipline is essential, what's important is the essence fueling discipline. On the very first day, we talked about coming to the practice with an intention of love, not in the hopes of becoming a better person because you're already wonderful.

Discipline is, at best, fueled by love. Not the stern taskmaster for whom perfect is never good enough, but the loving Earth mother who demands the best from you because she wants to see you thrive and blossom into your potential.

Those two types of fuel feel very different and can lead to different results.

The secret behind cultivating the kind of discipline that builds you up is to fuel it with devotion — devotion to your highest self, to your connection with the divine, God, the universe, whatever it is you believe, whatever it is that calls you to the practice.

From this space of devotion, you can't help but show up for yourself every day. Tap into the groundswell of energy that's greater than you and allow it to carry you to the practice every day, even when you don't want to.

As you connect to the infinite every day, fuel up with devotion, filling your tank so that you can live in accordance with your highest, best self. Because not showing up for meditation is not showing up for you. When you don't commit to being the best person you can be, you fall short of your destiny.

Your soul relies on your limited, finite self to make good decisions so that you can express your soul signature in this realm. You have a purpose and a duty to be your best self, and to show up in the world reflecting that self because the world needs the best version of you.

The best you is the version beneath the fear and the doubt and the resistance — all the things that block the radiance of your true self from shining through.

Complementing this devotion is gratitude, not only for the practice, but for you who continues to show up.

This practice will change your life. It tunes you into the source of all that is, allowing it to burn away everything that holds you back from living your greatness. Off the cushion, you will be tested. People will annoy you, problems will develop, you'll feel uncertain and sometimes full of doubt.

The gift of the practice is that no matter what happens on the outside, you can return here, to this place of stillness, and remember who you are.

Earlier this week, we talked about how it's not the biggest deal in the world to miss a day's practice. And when you look at meditation in this framework, considering the sacred, powerful, life-long practice that it truly is, the idea of beating yourself up for missing a day seems so silly.

Because the intention of the practice isn't about getting your worldly self to meet an arbitrary goal of meditating every day.

The essence of the practice is to allow your eternal self to expand until it's so big that it naturally influences your worldly self. You effortlessly feel more peace, compassion and love — all the things reflecting the truth of who you really are.

When you approach the practice this way, you'll have an easier time devoting yourself to it. You can meditate so that your life is better and you feel better about yourself.

But you can also meditate because the connection you feel in the stillness is your connection to life itself.

Journal prompts

If you were truly, overwhelmingly grateful for every single opportunity in your life, what value, idea, project or goal would you be most devoted to? What disciplines are necessary to cultivate that devotion? What fuels this devotion?

Integration

You're almost there! Stay strong over these last two days so you can walk over the finish line victorious.

It's time to truly own your practice by setting some intentions for how you want to continue now that the journal is ending.

Day 29: What is your dose?

Today, I invite you to review the past month or so and examine how you felt after various amounts of time spent in meditation, if the amount of time you practiced varied.

How long did you meditate on a typical day? How did it feel for you? Did you notice a difference on days when you practiced for a shorter or longer time?

As your practice deepens, you will naturally crave longer periods of time. You'll experience the benefits, the healing potential, and want more. Soon, when you feel emotional discomfort, your first inclination will be to sit with yourself, to feel.

It's a beautiful thing when your practice becomes your resting place, a space to process and heal.

For an everyday practice, you may wish to experiment and find an amount of time that works for you, not just in terms of your schedule, but in terms of how the practice makes you feel.

How do you feel when meditating 10 minutes a day, and how does that feeling compare to sitting for 15 or 20 minutes?

For me, meditating 10 minutes every day keeps me calm and present enough. But my optimal dosage is 20 minutes. With this length of time, I feel more connected and more capable of reflecting my higher self in all that I do. Thirty minutes makes me feel really good, but it's honestly too long for a daily practice and I end up skipping too many days. What works for you will be unique to you.

Not going to lie, it was a challenge building up to 20 minutes. When my mind hears that number, it immediately spirals into wondering how I'll make it through. I used to feel fear at sitting with myself for such a long time without fillers or filters. But over time, I've grown used to that mind chatter and it's easier to ignore.

I use the memory of how good it feels to emerge from a 20-minute practice to inspire the continued habit. Experiment and see what works for you. Once you find your optimal dosage, practice it daily.

Meditation is medicine

You may develop the habit of sitting every day, and then a difficult time comes to your life. Think of meditation as medicine. When you're sick with a fever or headache, you might take medicine to help you feel better.

Meditation can be your medicine for emotional pain, stress, doubt or confusion. When sadness or anger or uncertainty arises, create the habit of turning to the practice, possibly meditating more than you would normally. In the stillness, you'll find answers, solace and healing. In stillness, you process and heal.

Even if you don't lengthen your normal seated time, feel free to add in additional small pockets of peace during the day. Meditating an extra five minutes here, five minutes there all adds up. This intensified meditation time will give your heart and soul what it needs to process life circumstances and heal.

At various points in your life, you may wish to supercharge your spiritual journey, to break into the next level. Increasing the amount of time you spend meditating is a wonderful way to do that.

There is no book you can read, no teacher you can encounter that can substitute for the work of going within and sitting with all that arises, finding love for all that is.

Because there is no real backtracking in this journey, it's entirely possible to meditate for longer periods of time than usual and then return to your normal practice while still retaining that sense of spiritual evolution.

This is why meditation retreats and experiences like this are so good — they provide you not only with a deep connection during the journey, but the effects last for a long time.

Journal prompts

What is your optimal dosage of meditation? In times of trouble in your life, how do you normally cope? What patterns do you fall into? What would it take for you to respond in healthier ways? Create a plan for doing that.

Day 30: Preparing for success.

Welcome to the last day! Can you believe our time together is ending? Thank you so much for allowing me to guide your journey through these 30 days of meditation. I hope you have enjoyed this experience.

This last week has been full of integration tips because I know that leaving this cocoon of support can be a jarring transition. Today, I'll guide you through a series of questions to help you create a practice that works for you.

How to create a practice that works for you

1. Identify a time of day

What time has worked best for you throughout the past 30 days? Forgetting about when you think you should meditate, what time rises up from within as the best time to practice?

Thirty days is a great running start to implement the meditation habit, but know that this habit is like a seedling — sprouted, but not firmly rooted. Take care to water this seedling by meditating at the same time every day.

Once the habit is established, you will have more freedom to be flexible, but at the start, I encourage you to stick to a steady time of day.

2. Plan for obstacles

This is a critical element to establishing any new habit. Be realistic about the obstacles you'll face and then devise a way to overcome them. Do you like to snooze 800 times and oversleep, resulting in a rushed morning with no time to sit?

Overcome this obstacle by shifting something in your morning routine, maybe switching showering or picking out your outfit to the night before. Whatever is the morning's most time-consuming task, strategize ways to shave off even five minutes, creating time to meditate, if you choose to meditate in the morning.

This is the path of least resistance. It will be much easier for you to switch when you shower or how you eat breakfast rather than reducing the number of times you snooze. Select a habit you know you can change without much effort.

3. Cherish your vision

Take a moment to reflect on the positive changes you've experienced over the past 30 days of meditating. Thank yourself for investing the time, money and energy to develop this new habit. The person you were 30 days ago made a very important decision to make the rest of your life the best of your life.

Develop a vision going forward. Who do you want to be? How will meditation help you live that reality?

Every day, you make the choice to serve your future self by showing up to meditate. Allow this vision to inspire your daily dedication.

Writing things down is an important way to imprint this goal in your subconscious, so definitely write your vision in the journal spaces below.

4. Identify misconceptions of the practice

The past month has been a journey into your heart. Take a minute to review your time and identify any unhelpful ideas that came up about meditation or meditators.

Maybe you have a limiting belief that unless you meditate for 20 minutes a day, it's not worth doing. Perhaps, even more basic, you believe peace is for other people, but not you.

Change can also be scary. You may worry what will happen to your life as you become more conscious. Sometimes we stay small not because we enjoy it, but because it's comfortable. It's okay. Take some time to explore on what limiting beliefs and fears you have around the practice.

Often, limiting beliefs and fears can manifest in ridiculous excuses about why you can't meditate. Identify the fears and then you'll know when you're just making excuses to keep yourself small.

5. Reframe limiting beliefs

Write simple affirmative statements, again recruiting your subconscious mind to help you. Things like, "It's okay to meditate for only 5 minutes a day." "It's okay if I skip a day as long as I start again the next." Develop a new belief system — a belief system that will serve you as you become a life-long meditator.

6. Identify resistance to the practice itself

In what ways have you had to persuade yourself to practice over the past 30 days? If you skipped a lot of days, what was the cause of that? Be honest with yourself!

Go a little deeper: Are you afraid to sit with yourself? Are you afraid of creating space? Maybe even meditate on it and see what comes up! You could also free write and ask your higher self to give you insight.

7. Create new self-talk

How will you overcome your tricky mind tricks? You might remind yourself of your vision, or imagine how peaceful you'll feel after meditation.

This tool — using the memory of emotion to inspire your practice — is really effective. It allows you to come to the practice with love, and not a sense of feeling forced.

Identify at least one type of positive self-talk to keep yourself inspired to continue.

8. Create a plan

Take pieces from your answers above and combine them to create a vision of your ideal meditation practice and how you'll overcome obstacles. Even if you never refer to it again, the simple act of writing your plan down will help you stick to it.

Hopefully, you've seen first hand how much potential this habit offers you. It's my sincerest wish for you that you now take this practice and the tools you've learned to bring more mindfulness and peace into your daily life. May you love yourself more every day, and may you live as a force of love and goodness in the world.

Thank you so much for being here. Many blessings to you on your continued journey. Grateful to walk this road together.

Journal prompts

Answer the questions from today's reading!

You did it!

Thank you for showing up for yourself in a big way and making massive moves towards unleashing the most peaceful, powerful version of your true self.

Regardless of how many days you meditated, how many journal prompts you skipped or didn't skip, I know that the simple act of dedicating time and energy to yourself has shifted the energy within you.

I hope you feel more connected to your higher self and in tune with a more loving energy. It's now your sacred duty to continue the momentum that you've so diligently created for yourself. I know you can do it!

If you ever fall off track (we all do) simply begin again! No judgment needed. Every day is a new day to begin again.

The end!

Thank you so much for choosing Soul Scroll Journals as a guide through the galaxy of your inner world!

Our mission is to help you know, love and trust yourself so you can create a life as unique as you are.

We hope that you now feel more empowered to create a beautiful life of your choosing rather than the one you're programmed for or expected to live.

Please let us know how your experience was!

What's next:

1. Leave a review.

Did you love this journal? Share your thoughts on Amazon and let others know about your experience so their lives can also be transformed. This is how we change the world!

2. Download your bonus gifts at SoulScrollJournals.com/bonuses.

If you haven't already downloaded the Feeling Awareness meditation to help you connect to your heart and release painful emotions, go do that now!

3. Join the Soul Scroll Journal Family Facebook group!

Head to www.facebook.com/groups/soulscrolljournals to connect with others also on the path of creating an extraordinary life.

Everyone has a dream inside of them they're meant to live. Yet not everyone trusts themselves enough to create this dream and realize their destiny.

This is no small thing. The unique essence of you was created for a reason, and it will never exist again.

Too many people are held back because they don't know how to release past pain, find the answers within, and trust themselves to create the extraordinary life they're meant to live.

Too many people are so full of external information and well-meaning but ultimately noisy advice that they've lost connection to their own hearts.

We wanted to inspire dreamers to put down their phones and scroll their souls.

To find the vision within and connect to the heartfelt guidance to create it, one day at a time.

That's why Soul Scroll Journals were born. The journals are your friend and unbiased guide to help you connect to your heart, clarify your dreams and desires, and teach you how to use your intuition to create it.

They'll help you become the person you were always meant to be — right now.

Download a free, powerful meditation to release past pain and connect to your heart at SoulScrollJournals.com/bonuses.

Play with the Day yearly goal journal

Cast a vision. Set monthly intentions. Live with soul.
Play with the Day is a soulful goal journal and habit tracker that will help you live better — not just get more done.
With it, you'll weave beautiful rituals and habits into your life along with a few focused to-do's, leaving plenty of room for play.

Listen to Your Heart guided journal

Your heart is always guiding you to a life you love. This journal will help you hear these important messages.
Listen to Your Heart guided journal will support you through short daily readings and thought-provoking journal prompts to get crystal clear on what you want while releasing everything holding you back from creating it.

Self-Love guided journal

This journal is for people are tired of criticizing and doubting themselves and want to feel good enough.
You were born a unique, sparkly being of infinite potential. It's time to embrace who you really are! This guided journal will show you how.

Find these journals and more at SoulScrollJournals.com.

Made in the USA
Monee, IL
16 August 2021